W9-CHY-027

HOW TO ANALYZE HANDWRITING

HOW TO ANALYZE HANDWRITING

BY HAL FALCON, Ph.D.

Published by Galahad Books, New York, N.Y.

This book published with permission of

Simon & Schuster, Inc. New York, N.Y.

Library of Congress Catalog Card Number 73-80629

ISBN: 0-88365-068-1

Contents

Preface

"Whatever trait a person shows in his handwriting, he tends to show in every other action that is habitual." This is the author's basic tenet.

Generally, statements by the author are strictly empirical. He need not be modest about this; he is a good observer and can rely on what he sees, whether or not there is a theory to bear him out.

This book points out the importance of cooperation between members of the medical profession and graphologists. We are ironically told of graphologists who believe they can, via the expectant mother's subconscious and its expression in sex symbols, predict whether the child will be a boy or girl.

Falcon conjures the subconscious where physicians would avoid this expression. Where the author refers to Freudian mechanisms, physicians often speak of physiological processes not represented in consciousness.

The chapter on signatures is especially rewarding. There is an array of most interesting, easily observable facts of value to any reader, laymen as well as professional men.

W. G. Eliasberg, M.D., Ph.D.
Fellow, American Psychiatric Association
Fellow, New York Academy of Medicine
Life Fellow, American Medical Association
P. pres., American Society of Psychoanalytic Physicians
Hon. member, Allg. Ärztlichen Gesellschaft für Psychotherapie, Vienna, Austria

HOW TO ANALYZE HANDWRITING

Chapter 1. Handwriting Is An Action That Is Habitual

Handwriting is an action that is habitual.

Whatever trait a person shows in one type of action that is habitual, he tends to show in every other type of habitual action.

Therefore, whatever trait a person shows in his handwriting, he tends to show in every other action that is habitual.

This bit of logic is the principle on which every chapter in this book is based. It is the basic principle for analyzing handwriting which I have worked out during more than twenty years of experience; during these twenty years I have analyzed signatures, plus one or more written sentences, of at least 100,000 different individuals.

Are you one of those people who doesn't believe in handwriting analysis? "I don't believe in fortune-telling by handwriting," did I hear you say? Well, I don't believe in fortune-telling by handwriting, either. I am definitely *not* a fortune-teller, a seer, a mind-reader; I am not a prophet of the future. I am a "person-analyst" who obtains strictly scientific answers by applying proven psychological principles to the *movements* that a hand makes in the action of writing. The marks by the pen or pencil serve only to show what those movements were, just as the tracks left by his unseen prey tell an experienced hunter whether his quarry is wounded and limping, or walking, or running. If you will study all the chapters in this book, you will be able to make accurate statements concerning a person's traits just by analyzing his handwriting.

To illustrate this principle, let us assume that you are at a neighbor's house, watching some home movies he has made. In the pictures, you see a stranger hurrying down the street. So you comment to your neighbor: "That fellow must have been late for his train."

"No, no—that's Joe Smith," says your host. "He's always like that: walks fast, talks fast, eats fast, thinks fast, drives fast, or at least he did until he got a ticket for speeding last week." And, although your neighbor didn't mention it, you can bet that Joe Smith *writes* fast also.

Now let's just turn this sequence around: if we see a sample of writing that was obviously done with great speed, we can say: "This writer is a person who thinks fast, talks fast, walks fast, eats fast, and drives fast, unless he has had an attack of indigestion or a speeding ticket recently."

How then can you tell if the writing was done at a fast, slow, or medium speed? Certainly if you watch it being written, you can judge for yourself without having to use a stop watch, just as you can estimate whether a man walking down the street is walking fast or slowly without having to time him. (In a later chapter I will show you examples of writing done at different speeds, and I will point out the details by which you can tell whether the hand movements were fast or slow.)

In order to learn about a person's sex interests from his handwriting, we can use two basic concepts strongly emphasized by the Freudian school of psychologists: the female symbol and the phallic one. The phallic symbol occurs most often in the letters *y* and *g*, although I have seen it in other letters, such as *l, d, s,* and *C.*

1-1

Figure 1-1 is a diagram I made of a fictitious name, "M. N. Collins," because I would consider the elongated loops on the *C* and *s* as phallic symbols, especially if the rest of the writing repeated them; and the woman whose signature is the basis for this one did repeat them in her *y* and *g*. Her name was *not* "Collins," but it did have loops like these, one on an initial and one on a terminal *s*.

If you are old enough to read this chapter, you probably know that Sigmund Freud and his followers, in interpreting dreams as a part of psychoanalysis, considered that a snake, a furled umbrella, a walking-stick, an arrow or spear, or various similar objects, usually represented the male sex organ. Now if you will refer to the diagram of the word "bay" immediately preceding Figure 6-1 in chapter 6 you will see that the base line of the writing correlates with the crotch. This correlation makes it obvious why *y* and *g* are the letters that most often show this phallic symbol and why the symbol occurs in the name "Collins" at the points where you see it. In other specimens that I will show you later, the letters *d* and *l* have attached to them below the base line an extra tail, similar to that of the *g* in the same script—a most unusual formation which each writer used twice.

As for symbols representing the female, the Freudian suggest darkness, softness, fur, a cave, and many others. The triangle, which the Freudians do not mention, frequently appears in handwriting as a female symbol. Usually it does not rest on a side, but stands on a point, thus being a picture or diagram of the largest area of pubic hair on the female body. At least 99 percent of the number of times that it appears, the triangle is in the tail of a terminal *y* or *g*. Theoretically it could occur in other letters with tails, such as *f, j, p, q,* and *z,* but I have rarely found it in these letters, perhaps because few words in English end with any of them; in other languages the situation might be different. Thus, my own study of handwriting leads me to believe firmly that the triangle is a female symbol, made by the subconscious as a picture of the shape of the area of pubic hair.

Let me tell you a teen-age love story. At least, Rollo and Julie (these are not their real names, of course) were very young teen-agers when it started, but both were old enough to vote when I met them in my usual manner, by analyzing their handwriting.

I was working that summer in Southhampton on Long Island, giving lectures in the famous Bowden Square Restaurant run by the fabulous Herb McCarthy, who had been my earliest sponsor when I first arrived in New York City in 1950. Rollo was spending a final week there with his parents before leaving for his senior year at a well-known university in a nearby state.

He wrote for me the sample you see here (Figure 1-2); because of the misspelling, I explained that I thought he was ear-minded, had good pitch discrimination, and could be fluent in languages. He said that these points were precisely correct, and he had had enough psychology at college to be surprised at my getting them from his writing.

Because his *g* was unusually long and there was a rounded triangle in his *y,* I told him he possessed an unusually strong sex urge that was completely starved at the moment. Again he said this was accurate and demanded to know how I could tell it from his writing. When I pointed out the phallic and the female symbol for him and explained that the long, long space from the base line to the point where the return curve crossed the downstroke on the tail of the *g* meant that subjectively he felt that "it had been a long, long time," he had enough knowledge of Freud to understand instantly.

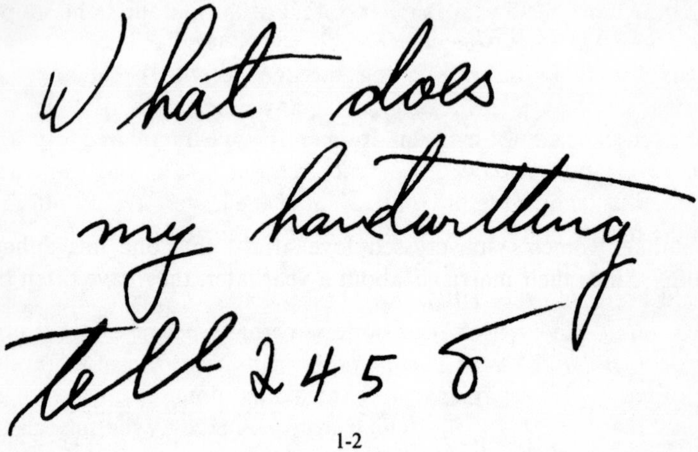

1-2

"Man, oh man! Are you ever *right,* professor!" Rollo said. "My fiancée's been in Bermuda for a month with her family and it seems like a year! But if you think I'm passionate, wait till you see *her* writing! I know I'm oversexed, sure, but she's enough for two men like me! I'm going to look at some of the letters she wrote me and see what her *y* and *g* look like. And I'll tell you what, she's landing at Kennedy tomorrow noon, so I'll bring her in to see you tomorrow night. Let's see what her writing says about it!"

He did bring her in, just as promised. They came so late in the evening that the restaurant was almost deserted; we sat at a table in an empty corner while I talked with them. She frankly confirmed the opinion he had expressed of her, that she was extraordinarily passionate; and together, bit by bit, they told me the details of their story.

On their second date they had started "honeymooning," as they called it, and had repeated the sex experience at every opportunity that offered sufficient privacy; but opportunity had never knocked often enough to keep her really happy. While still in prep school, Rollo had somehow obtained a copy of the *Kama Sutra,* a suppressed book about sexual practices in the Far East of a century or more ago. They had experimented, using it as a textbook, trying to duplicate every activity described that required only two participants.

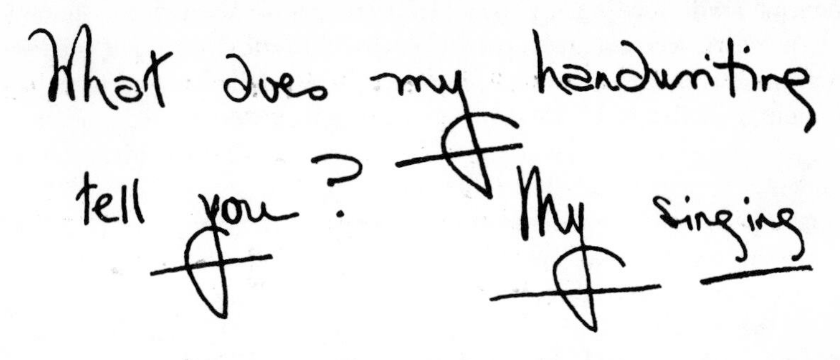

1-3

Unlike Romeo's star-crossed love affair, this one has a happy ending. Since their marriage, about a year later, they have often been in to see me together, usually when celebrating some particular event, such as the day Rollo received word he had passed the bar examination. In view of their differences, Julie being very much the oversexed one, this particular couple, having much intelligence and a great deal of luck, apparently solved for themselves a very troublesome problem Nature had thrust upon them. The last time I saw them was on the occasion of their tenth wedding anniversary, and they proudly showed me pictures of their three children.

Evidence of sexual frustration among teen-agers in our population is not uncommon. The problem arises from the fact that puberty and the sex urge that goes with it come a dozen or so years after birth, but the average age for marriage (in the United States at present) is another dozen years later and, as far as the men are concerned, the ability to support a wife and family may not arrive for almost another dozen. Our puritanical civilization offers a young man only two rules to guide him through this difficulty: (1) don't marry until you can support a family, and (2) remain completely continent until after you are married (this second precept is preached over and over again to our girls). I doubt if these rules are easy for as many as 20 percent of our population, and certainly at the other end of the scale we have at least 20 percent for whom the inborn sex urge is at least as strong as the alcoholic's desire for his next drink or the chain smoker's for his next cigarette.

Now let's go back to the phrase "tends to" in our first paragraph: ". . . whatever trait a person shows in his handwriting, he *tends* to show in every other action that is habitual." If you are looking for mathematical exactness in handwriting analysis, you won't find it. But then, you will not find it in any other test that deals with the human mind, either. For example, the oldest psychological test now used in this country, the one for determining the I.Q. (intelligence quotient), is the Binet-Simon test, which originated in France in 1905 and was brought here in 1916 by the late Dr. Lewis M. Terman of Stanford University, who revised and developed it extensively. Its variation from accuracy is considered to be ±5 percent.

Furthermore, if you are ill or suffering from fatigue or emotional distress when you take such a test, these factors may cause your score to be substantially lower than it would be otherwise. Also, it is my opinion that this and other forms of intelligence tests, such as the Wechsler-Bellevue, give an undue handicap to that 40 percent of the U.S. population who are *not* eye-minded. Later chapters in this book are devoted to eye-minded, ear-minded, and action-minded individuals; precise instructions are given telling you how to identify each type by his or her handwriting.

The Hermann Rorschach test, which uses the ten standardized inkblots, has been well validated, but even when used by a qualified expert its results average only 85 percent accuracy. The T.A.T. (Thematic Apperception Test) and the word-association test (made famous by Carl G. Jung) give no better percentages.

The L.S.A.T. (Law Students Aptitude Test), used by Ivy League universities as a basis for determining admissions to their law colleges, shows good correlation with the scholarship ranking of graduating students who had previously taken it. However, in almost every class there are students who flunk out although their test scores indicated they could be honor graduates. On the other hand, it often occurs that a student who barely gets in, because of a low L.S.A.T. score, will finish among the top 5 percent of his class.

In contrast to this, handwriting analysis, when used by competent graphologists for personnel work, has attained a proven record of 93 percent accuracy.

So if you will apply properly the basic principles in all the chapters of this book, *you* can get 80 percent to 90 percent accuracy in stating a writer's personal traits, just by studying for a few minutes a specimen of his ordinary writing. The chapters that follow discuss, one by one, the various characteristics you can learn from such analysis and tell you where to look for personality traits in any sample of writing.

Now it is true that graphology (this is the name for the science of describing personality and talents by analysis of handwriting) will not tell you if the writer has blue eyes or brown, if he is tall, short, thin, or fat, or if he has had sixty birthdays or only thirty. But what it does tell, it reveals with remarkable ease and accuracy, if you will just stick to the basic principles stated in this book.

This consistency in "the pattern of habitual action" is the first fact I ever learned about handwriting analysis, and I stumbled upon it quite by accident. When I first became a graduate student, I earned "rent money" by grading papers and running a weekly quiz hour as "reader" for an English professor. Each week I corrected and graded what seemed like acres of handwritten themes and tests.

By accident I noticed that when I gave a written test, certain students always finished long before the others. When I gave an oral quiz, these same students stood up rapidly to recite, spoke quickly, sat down immediately, and when the bell rang, they were the first ones out the door.

Certain others were just the opposite: they wrote so slowly that they rarely finished a written test; in reciting, they rose slowly from their seats, spoke slowly, took their seats slowly; and at the end of the hour they strolled out the door in a leisurely manner.

As an undergraduate with a minor in psychology, I had studied *Behavior: An Introduction to Comparative Psychology,* by Dr. John B. Watson of Johns Hopkins (Henry Holt & Co., New York, 1914), so to me it was noteworthy that these students showed a pattern of behavior that was consistent, even in the several different actions of moving, talking, walking, and writing. Although up to that time I had never even heard the word "graphologist" and most certainly I never expected to become one, it did seem fascinating that the speed or slowness in writing, as I saw it in the classroom, was evident also in other actions of the same person. It occurred to me that there must be other correlations as well, and I began to look for them.

Before long I discovered that the athletes—and there were many student athletes in those classes, because journalism and commercial English were considered "crip" courses—wrote with pressure that was noticeably heavy as compared with that of other students. In chapter 5 I will tell you in detail about differing amounts of pressure in handwriting because the traits you can discover from this one factor are quite important. For instance, the normal writing of a man who is successful in any field that involves selling or sales management—including not only canvassing and direct selling, but advertising, merchandising, marketing, fund raising, publicity, and public relations—invariably shows heavy pressure. Often the pressure is so marked that I have had to discard the next two pages under the one on which the writing was done.

Over later years I discovered, by means of hundreds of examples, that the "subconscious mind" puts diagrams or pictures into handwriting that can be interpreted to obtain knowledge, sometimes including facts unknown even to the writer himself. I prefer the term "subconscious mind" to the word "unconscious" (as used by Werner Wolff, Thea Stein-Lewinson, and other writers on the subject of handwriting) because the "unconscious" suggests to me and to most people a state, similar to a faint or a coma, that simulates death. I am convinced that what I call the "subconscious" *never* becomes "unconscious" in the sense of being asleep or in a coma, while life exists, but that it is only the *conscious* mind that can be rendered "unconscious" by sleep or anaesthesia or otherwise.

Furthermore, I believe that this subconscious mind constantly strives to communicate to the conscious mind, somewhat as an intelligent five-year-old child born without vocal cords might strive to communicate. For example, in regard to sex: the subconscious habitually puts into a person's writing a great deal of information about his interest in sex and his sexual activities, or lack of these.

In general, if you do not have a great amount of sex urge yourself, you are not likely to have much appeal to the opposite sex, although it is certainly possible for a woman to have a voluptuous body and yet be, as the song writers put it, a "hard-hearted Hannah" with a "cold, cold heart." On the other hand, my clients have included a few women who were "very much oversexed" (for two of them, this was an official diagnosis made by the family doctor) but who unfortunately lacked much of the external appearance that arouses male interest.

If you have teen-agers in your family, or if you deal with them through Scouting or Boys' Clubs or other teaching or counseling, this chapter will show you how you can learn from their handwriting just which ones have a sex urge so strong as to be very troublesome. I have no solution to offer; but I do want to point out that persons who have these characteristics are no more responsible for possessing them than they are for the color of their eyes. Nature provides glands that produce certain chemicals; if the quantity is large, the great urge that ensues is natural and inevitable. Conscious application of willpower cannot eliminate the desires these hormones create.

Figures 1-4, 1-5, and 1-6 are copies of the writing of three men,

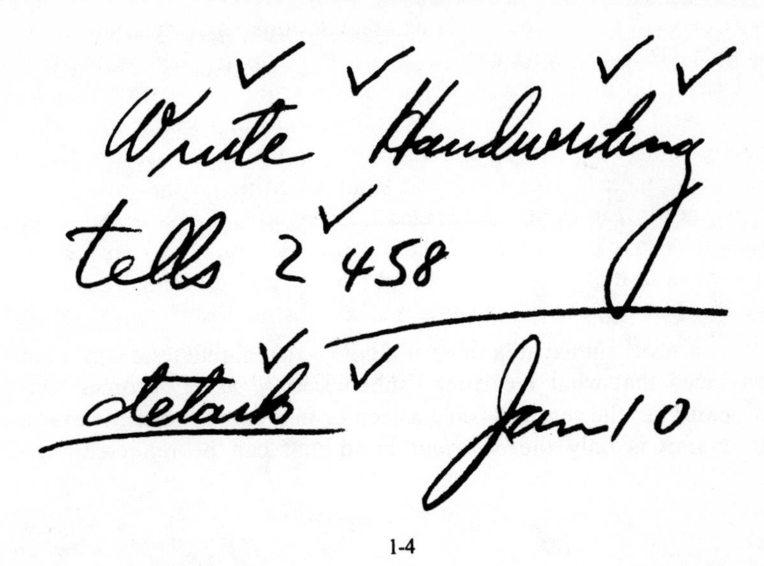

1-4

each of whom said he had had a tremendous sex urge ever since puberty or even before. Look at the *g,* which in each case has a length (as measured from its highest point to its lowest) at least twice as great as the height of the *h, d, t,* or *l* in the same script. The first two men are business executives; the third is a very successful traveling salesman. You can see that they are all action-minded, in sex as well as in commerce.

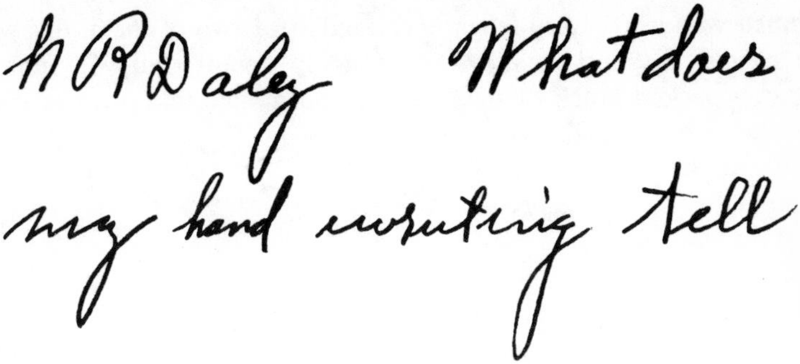

1-5

Old school graphologists say the sign of a talkative person is an *a* with a gap in its top or a *t* with a wide loop (so it resembles an *l* with a crossbar)—the space in each letter symbolizing "the open mouth." My experience has led me to disagree with this interpretation. It so happens that the salesman in this last group of men insisted on discussing his own faults as well as his other traits; in his opinion his worst fault was that he was too talkative, both socially and when calling on his customers. Certainly our interview confirmed this fact: I was being paid to talk, but I had trouble getting in one word to his five. Yet his *a* in each word is closed up tightly, as you can see, and the only *t* that has an open loop is in *writing*—but this space is tiny compared to the space in the *l* that he wrote several times. The letters *a* and *t* also appear in his name and are just as firmly "shut" as the ones pictured here. If this man's writing does contain any indication that he is overly talkative, it does not lie in the letters *a* and *t*.

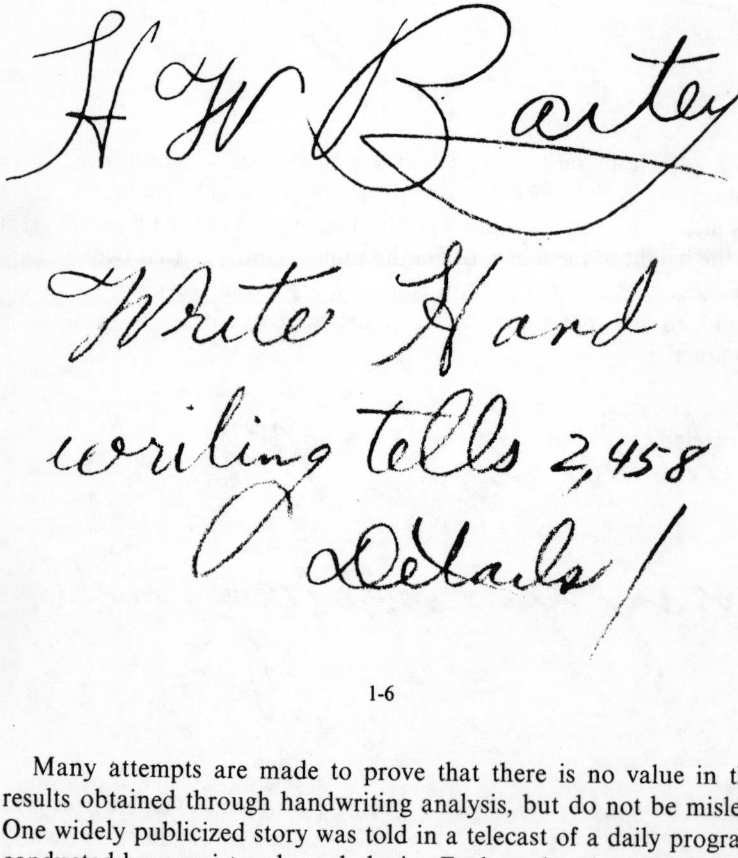

1-6

Many attempts are made to prove that there is no value in the results obtained through handwriting analysis, but do not be misled. One widely publicized story was told in a telecast of a daily program conducted by a registered psychologist. Each student in a psychology class at a university was shown a somewhat vague, generalized, and slightly flattering description of personality which—so the instructor said—had been obtained through an analysis of the pupil's handwriting. Each pupil acknowledged the accuracy with which he had been described, unaware that in reality he was reading the same report that had been shown to every one of the others. According to the registered psychologist running the television show, this incident proved that graphology has no validity at all.

The fallacy, as you must have observed, is that the description of personality used had nothing whatever to do with handwriting analysis; the instructor only *said* it had been made by means of graphology. If he had used exactly the same procedure with a different class, telling them the delineation was based on an ink-blot test, he could have proved just as effectively that the Rorschach has no validity. Then, one by one, he could have told other classes that the description was based on, respectively, a Stanford Binet, a Wechsler-Bellevue, a Minnesota Multiphasic, an A.V.A., a personnel interview, or any other test they had ever heard of; and thus within a single week he could have "disproved" the value of every appraisal method known to modern psychology.

So, insofar as this particular story is concerned, "Methinks he doth protest too much."

The newspapers, too, take a hand in spreading this sort of misinformation. One account which I read recently, which was directed against the "personality test," said that about seventy personnel directors, gathered at a management conference at Wayne University in Detroit, had themselves been subjected to one of the many tests that are frequently used on job applicants. Afterward, each man was given just such a "vague, generalized description," but the professor had it individually typed for each delegate and properly labeled with each man's name and company at the top of the page to make it more convincing. As usual, each man was told it was an official evaluation based on the personality form he had completed, and each one accepted it as applying to himself; a few even praised it for the exceptional insight it showed.

However, this time (if the news story is correct) the description was actually based on a report written by an astrologer for a client who had consulted him about a horoscope and its meaning. By adding this new element to the experiment, the Wayne University professor could claim that he killed two birds with one stone: he had disproved the validity both of astrology and of personality tests, or so he could *say*.

Again, the fallacy is that the description used really had no relationship to the actual test that had been given; the professor only *said* that it was an evaluation of such a test.

So remember this above all: in analyzing a specimen of handwriting, mention only those traits that are clearly revealed. At first you might even limit yourself to mentioning traits for which you can point out indications in the handwriting.

For instance, if every *i* is dotted, every *t* is crossed, every capital and every mark of punctuation in the original is properly reproduced in a person's script, he can observe this fact once you have pointed it out to him. If the pressure is light, moderate, or heavy, this again is something he can see for himself, especially if you have other specimens with which to compare his. If he writes very fast, or very slowly, he can realize this once you mention it. If he makes phonetic misspelling of words in the copy; if his writing shows gaps between the letters or has connecting "garlands" forming a rhythmic base line; or if he writes an engineer's 4 and 8, an accountant's 2 and 5, or a German *H* and *t,* all these facts will be obvious to him as well as to everyone else who is present when you cite them.

If, then, you will interpret these undeniable facts according to the principles described in later chapters, no professor in any university in the world can successfully contradict either your facts or your interpretation of them. It is better to make only five such interpretations, and to be indubitably correct in all of them, than to make a "vague, generalized description" that mentions fifty possible traits that might fit anybody.

If you hammer home with conviction just five definite characteristics, each fully supported by details you have pointed out to him and have interpreted according to the principles in this book, your subject will have to acknowledge your accuracy, no matter how skeptical he may have been originally. He will be both surprised and pleased, and it will be your experience, as it has been mine, that he will remember your accuracy for years. In fact, chances are he will continue to praise you to his friends even after he has forgotten the precise five points that you scored truly in your analysis.

The real problem for me now is one of selectivity. Often I see two or three dozen characteristics in one person's script that I could talk about. Within the time allotted for the interview I usually discuss and explain only the ten or twelve traits that seem most important under the circumstances. For example, if a woman who had never had a job should consult me about the kind of work for which she was best suited, the things I would tell her would be quite different from the ones I would discuss if her fiancé brought me exactly the same specimen of her writing and asked me whether she would be a suitable wife for him. But in both analyses I would be entirely sincere and professionally correct in any statement that I made.

When you have had experience in using the information given in this book, you will yourself be able to analyze handwriting specimens accurately; and as you do, always keep in mind this proven principle: *Whatever trait a person shows in one type of action that is habitual, such as the movement of the hand in writing, he tends to show in every other type of habitual action.*

Chapter 2. How To Prepare A Good Handwriting Specimen

If you want to analyze your own handwriting, you must first have a good specimen of it to examine. A letter or memo—say a grocery or laundry list—will do, but since you plan to make a psychology test, I suggest you make a new sample for just this purpose.

The results of your analysis will be much more accurate if you control the conditions under which you make your handwriting sample. In this chapter the best conditions for attaining accuracy are described. Every single word stated is important for reasons you will learn later in this book, so follow the instructions very carefully.

You understand, of course, that if someone gives you for analysis a letter or other specimen, such as an envelope or a postcard with writing on it, you must do the best you can under the circumstances. Similarly, a detective, seeking clues to a crime, must study even a smudged fingerprint, or a half of one, but if he is taking prints for study, he will control meticulously the details as to the ink, the paper, and the method of making the specimen. You should be just as meticulous in making your own sample to be analyzed.

Here are the rules:

1) PLEASE BE SEATED. Sit at a steady table or desk large enough for you to rest your whole forearm on it from elbow to wrist. Be sure the height from the floor of both the table or desk top and the chair seat are correct for your comfort, both separately and in relationship to each other. *Do not write* while standing or with the paper on a board or magazine in your lap or on a wobbly table or desk: the wobbles will show in your writing.

2) PAPER. Use blank paper with no printing or lines on it, preferably a 16- or 20-pound bond, not smaller than *half* the size of typewriter paper, which measures 8½ by 11 inches. *Do not use* wrapping paper, blotter, tissue paper, or the onion skin or other thin sheets typists use for carbon copies. Do not write on a correspondence

card, postcard, or postal or Bristol board. Be sure that under the page on which you write you have at least three or four sheets of paper of the same thickness as the one you are writing on.

3) PEN OR PENCIL. If you habitually use a certain fountain pen, use that; otherwise get a pencil with a sharp point, preferably a #1. If you use a drawing pencil, an indelible pencil, a #2 or harder pencil, or if you use a crayon, a carpenter's pencil, a drafting pen, a stylus, or a ball point pen, then you will not be able to analyze traits indicated by the various pressures in your writing.

4) SIGNATURE. Write your name the way you usually sign it; if you have a bank account, the form you put on your checks is probably your most natural one. Now look at the signature. If you spelled out any given name or used an abbreviation such as "Chas." or "Thos." or "Wm.," then write your name a second time using only an initial for each of your given names and including your last name in full. If you have only one given name but you sometimes approve or acknowledge a memo by putting on it your initials or a monogram or an "OK" followed by one or more initials, then write that form also.

5) TEXT. The following sentence contains four words and a number. As naturally as you can, write (or print if you usually print instead of write) each of the first three words, then the number, and the last word. Here is the sentence:

Write: Handwriting tells 2,458 details!

If you printed or lettered this sentence or wrote "manuscript" style, then write it again in cursive script. Or if you have two or more styles of writing (for instance, one backhand and one either vertical or inclined to the right), write the same sentence (including all four words and the number in its proper place) in one of the other different styles you use.

Now if you have written the sentence only once, write out any one of the following sentences:

a) The sly brown fox jumped over the lazy dog.
b) This style of writing is a display of the way I normally do it.
c) Today there is hardly time for every good man to aid his party.

Now that you have finished writing in accord with the above instructions, leave your sample as it is; don't go back and make any changes or erasures either now or as you read the later chapters. If, as you do read them, you mark any imperfections or mistakes with an arrow or checkmark, do so with a different pencil or pen, such as one that writes red or blue, and be careful that such markings do not touch or cross any line of your original copy.

As you read each chapter you will see why each of the details in the above instructions is important, and you will understand why I state them orally, one at a time, to every client who asks me to analyze his writing.

Keep your specimen handy so that you can study it as you read the following chapters. Are you eye-minded? Ear-minded? Action-minded? Does your writing limp? Is it filled with sex symbols? Read on and learn!

Chapter 3. Are You Eye-Minded?

If you are right-handed or left-handed or equal-handed (ambidextrous), this characteristic, it is now believed, was determined before you were born. When I was a first-grader, this was not considered to be a fact; the theory then was that a left-hander had merely started picking up things with his left hand instead of his right when an infant, and nobody had bothered to teach him better habits. In those days teachers often forced such pupils to hold the pencil in the right hand when learning to write. It is now understood that the frustration arising from such interference and the resulting awkwardness can produce serious nervous or emotional distress, such as stammering or stuttering in later years.

Now every normal person is born with eyes, ears, and muscles. For some people, the preferred method of learning is through the eye; for others, through the ear; and for still others, through use of the muscles. It has been estimated that approximately 60 percent of the U.S. population are eye-minded or visual-minded, 30 percent are ear-minded or auditory types, and the remaining 10 percent are action-minded or kinaesthetic.

Since the perfume industry boasts a few experts who can distinguish unbelievably small amounts of substances by their smell, and certain other industries employ tea tasters, coffee tasters, or wine tasters as experts in their particular fields, there must be people who are nose-minded or taste-minded; but these are so few in number that all of them put together wouldn't amount to a half of 1 percent of the population. If there is any possible method of spotting such talent by handwriting, I have not yet found it!

But there is a method by which you can look at the writing of a thousand different people and pick out, with at least 95 percent accuracy, those who are visual-minded. Of what use is this?

If you were a personnel director hiring people to do bookkeeping, filing, stenography, or other tasks requiring accurate reading of words and figures, it would save you hiring many wrong people. To put a man who is primarily ear-minded or action-minded on a job such as bookkeeping would only produce frustration on the part of both employer and employee.

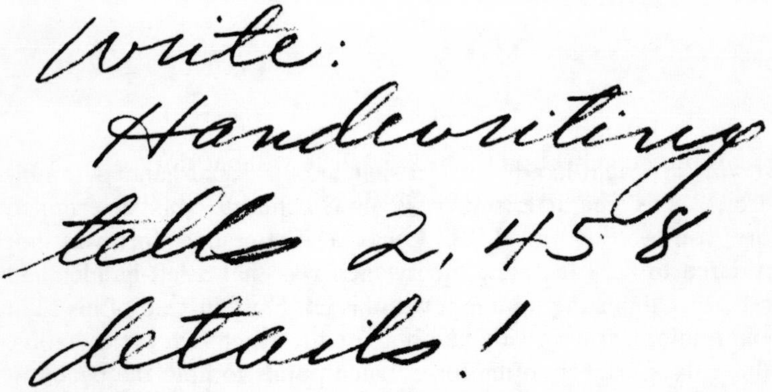

3-1 Visual-minded memory whiz who won over $100,000 on quiz shows, although he had little schooling.

Dr. Roscoe Pound, dean of Harvard Law School for twenty years, was born with such poor eyesight that from the day he started school he realized he would never be able to study by reading and re-reading a textbook. So when he entered law school he forced himself to memorize at first reading every single page he had to study. Years later he gave a series of lectures in England where he quoted page after page of decisions, citing cases by naming the book and the page on which the reference would be found. In making hundreds of such numerical references, he made only one mistake, citing a certain page as, let us say, number 243 when it should have been number 248. But when researchers looked up the book he had actually studied they found that the printer had used a broken type so that what should have been 8 actually looked like 3.

Dean Pound is an extreme case of a person with visual memory, but a visual memory is characteristic of eye-minded people whether their vision is normal or less than normal. Dean Pound was born with only 25 percent or less of what would be considered normal vision.

Inventor Thomas A. Edison also had a fantastically sharp visual memory. It is said that he could look for some sixty seconds at a page, such as one in an encyclopedia, and then, closing the book, he could call off the last word of every line, reading from either the top or the bottom of the page, or recite the entire page either forward or backward.

To possess a memory so accurate is a mark of genius; whereas if you are eye-minded you may possess this type of memory even though it is not nearly so accurate. For example, if you should ever happen to forget how to spell a difficult or unfamiliar word, you can write it down and look at what you have written; if it looks right, then it probably is spelled right. Or you may want to look up an article that you saw several days ago in a newspaper or magazine. You remember that it was in the upper right corner of the left-hand page, so you skim through the periodical and find the article without difficulty. If you have had such experiences you are obviously eye-minded, and this trait will show in the way you write.

To illustrate, let me tell you about just one of hundreds of such cases that I have found in my work. This man was a little over forty years old, and he had started more than twenty years earlier as a clerk in the office of a huge insurance company. When I met him to analyze his writing, he was the company's office manager, with quite a substantial salary, and had over 200 girls and men under his supervision. But the clatter of typewriters and adding machines was torture to him, and having to sit at a desk all day was as painful as solitary confinement for eight hours would be to most people. It is not surprising that he had been treated for ulcers on several occasions and was on the verge of becoming an alcoholic. At home, he confided, his wife and children found him so irritable that they spent as little time with him as possible.

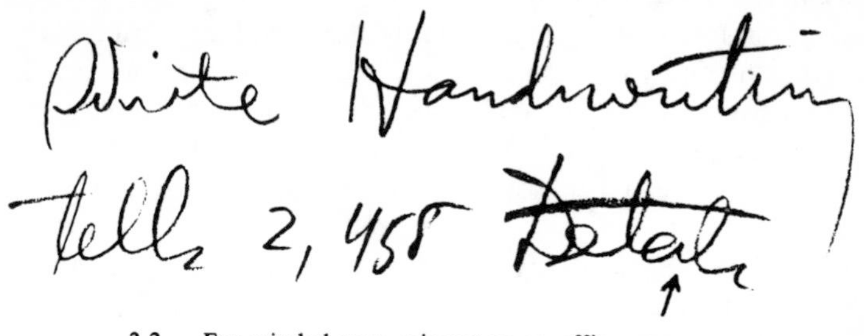

3-2 Ear-minded man miscast as an office manager.

Before he told me any of this, I had discovered that he was ear-minded, with action as his secondary talent, and his eyes (despite the 20/20 vision that he claimed) came in a poor third. Naturally I suggested that he had both musical and athletic activities in his past and that he should try to avoid paper work such as bookkeeping. When I finished my analysis, he told me that he had wanted to be a concert violinist, had spent several years of study and practice, and had been good enough on his high school football team to be offered free tuition at a big university.

But his family was not well off, so his parents had insisted on his taking a "regular" job as soon as he finished high school, and the first job he found was with the insurance company's office force. By sheer willpower and competitive drive he had forced himself to succeed in a field in which he was basically awkward, but his ulcers, his drinking, and his ill-temper were all part of the price he was paying for the strain and frustration of achieving that success.

Another similar case was that of a spinster whose writing I analyzed. From her appearance I judged her to be about sixty years of age. Her writing showed her to be strongly eye-minded and highly intelligent. I told her she was meticulous, cautious, analytical and that she would do quite well as an office manager, a schoolteacher, a librarian, or perhaps as an editor. She asked me if I thought she could be successful as a singer.

Since her voice showed anxiety over the question, I answered her as gently as I could: "If you have such talent, it does not show in *this* sample of your writing."

Immediately she burst into tears. After she was more composed, I asked what was troubling her.

"Your analysis is quite correct. I am doing exactly what you said," she told me. "I have a responsible job that is very well paid. I am chief librarian for a big recording company and I have dozens of girls working for me. Our library contains thousands of samples of the recordings made by our company and our competitors. We have lots of mansucripts and sheet music and thousands and thousands of cards that cross-index all these. In ten years I have been chief librarian, we have never lost a single record." She paused to wipe away a few tears.

"Well, then," I said, "why are you so distressed at my analysis?"

"Because I am a grand opera singer," she said. (I noticed she said specifically "I am" and not "I was" or "I wanted to be.") "I spent twenty years studying singing. My father was born in Italy. His father, his mother, and his grandfather were all singers. It was his ambition to be a grand opera star himself. But soon after he came to this country as a teen-ager, he got married, and then I came along, and there wasn't enough money for him to support a family and continue his music. But he soon did very well in his business, so I had singing lessons from the time I was three years old. Later I studied in Italy, Vienna, France, and Germany."

"And did you have a successful career in music?" I asked. This started more tears, and later:

"No, I never appeared in any part. I never even gave a single concert. I never quite thought I was good enough for that. I guess I am a perfectionist, just as you said. Unless I felt I could sing really, really well, I was afraid to face an audience at all. Then my father died and I had to take a job with this company as a file clerk to help support my mother and myself. I've been with them for years and years, and they think I am quite successful. But I don't want to be a librarian—I am a grand opera singer."

3-3 Chief librarian, who had wanted to be a grand opera prima donna.

If some competent graphologist had looked at this woman's handwriting when she was ten to fifteen years old, he could have saved her father thousands of dollars and saved her from years of wasted work and heartache by urging her to get into a field where she could use her major talent, her visual-mindedness. Today, I would urge such a girl to take the Seashore Musicality Test, but I don't think it had been established by the time she was ready for high school. However, even when she was ten, her father could have had her tested for pitch discrimination, and the low score that would have resulted would have proved she lacked sufficient talent for a career in music.

My third case on this subject is a success story of a man who learned his limitations—or perhaps I should say learned his true talents—and was able to make them work *for* him. When I analyzed his handwriting, I emphasized coordination as his major talent and praised his ear for music as his next most important one. Because of the pressure in his writing, I named competitive spirit and energy as third on the list and told him he must have been an outstanding athlete when he was of high school and college age and could have been good at such sports as rifle shooting, drop kicking, and pitching. I added that his "musical ear" was good enough that he could have learned to play any of several melodic instruments, such as the saxophone or the violin. On the negative side, I told him he disliked paper work so much that he should avoid all possible recording of expense accounts, financial statements, or tax reports. I spent fifteen to twenty minutes describing his traits, in descending order of importance: (1) kinaesthetic coordination, (2) pitch discrimination, (3) energy or "drive," and (4) visual perception (his *physical* vision was not poor; he said his eyesight was 20/20 and he never used glasses.)

3-4 Strongly coordinated musician; now a famous eye surgeon.

After I had finished my analysis and returned the paper with his writing on it, I sat and chatted with him and his wife for about a half hour. They confessed that, by agreement, they had asked no questions and made no comments at all during my talk because they were sure I would be able to tell them only facts gleaned from their conversation; to prevent this, they had maintained complete silence. But our later discussion proved that the graphology had been so accurate even I was a little surprised. Much of what I do know about handwriting I have learned from just such discussions about traits with persons whose writing I have first analyzed.

The man said he was a physician, chief of surgery for a hospital in upstate New York, and a lecturer in surgery at a university associated with it. His wife interrupted to say that his fame as an eye surgeon was so great that physicians from other states not only sent him patients, they came themselves to learn by watching him operate. Music was his hobby; he played several instruments by ear. He had spent hundreds of dollars for hi-fi and stereo equipment and the records and tapes to go with it; he had played violin in his high school orchestra; and he and his wife were at that moment in New York City to attend a couple of concerts and see some opera at the Met, as they usually did when he could get a brief vacation.

Point by point he confirmed numerous specific things I had told him in the analysis. As captain of the all-state football team his last year in high school, he had won a scholarship to the university, where he excelled in drop kicking, punting, and forward passing. He had been pitcher on the varsity baseball team and captain of the rifle shooting team. Scholastically he had done so well that he became a member of both Phi Beta Kappa and, later, its equivalent in medical colleges, Alpha Omega Alpha. As a physician he was a Fellow of several learned societies.

"I found out very early in my school days that I couldn't learn anything by reading a textbook," he told me. "I got through high school and college by listening carefully to what was said in class and making a few brief notes as an outline. That night, before I went to sleep, I wrote out in longhand exactly what had been said, as nearly as I could remember it. It was almost as if I had had a tape recorder in my brain. No matter how late I had to stay up, I *had* to write it out before I went to sleep or by the next day most of it would be forgotten. Somehow, the action of writing it fixed it in my brain; I never had to look at it again. I never had to 'cram' for an examination. Once I had written it out in longhand, it was there, ready any time I needed it. If there was a page in the textbook I had to learn, I read it out loud to myself, and then that evening I wrote it out in longhand just as if it had been a professor's lecture. If I read it silently even twenty times, I couldn't remember ten words of it, but if I read it out loud and then wrote it out, I remembered it from then on."

He said his hobbies, other than music, involved accuracy: he mentioned billiards, quail hunting, and skeet shooting.

Here is a case of a man who discovered accidentally what a few hours of aptitude testing or a few minutes of graphology, applied before he entered high school, could have told him more easily: that he was first action-minded and secondarily ear-minded (to use the terms in this book) and that he was so far from being visual-minded that he would have trouble remembering things he read. He was just plain lucky that he stumbled on a method that used the three main paths to his brain: the *action* of writing, the *sound* of the lecture or the reading aloud, and (least important to him) the *sight* of the words he had written out. But how many other potentially brilliant surgeons or musicians have flunked out of college or high school because the only method of learning that they were taught was learning by eyesight from textbooks?

Our entire school system is based on visual testing of visual-minded students taught by visual-minded instructors from textbooks prepared by visual-minded professors. This system handicaps the 40 percent of our population who are ear-minded or action-minded. Many of the aptitude tests in use today, including especially the intelligence tests, are open to the same criticism.

You can see now the importance of learning early in an individual's life whether he is visual-minded. But the question is: how can you tell from his writing?

Write = Handwriting
tells 2,458 details!

3-5 Visual-minded actress; usually among "ten best dressed" women each year; now star on her own TV show.

The answer is simple, logical, and in accord with just plain common sense. You ask your subject to write out, as naturally as he can, a sentence or two or three, containing a large number of visual details, such as commas, semicolons, quotation marks, capital letters, *i*-dots, *t*-crosses, and perhaps a few words that are easily misspelled. If he copies a paragraph, putting in correctly all these details, then he is eye-minded. The more mistakes he makes, the more likely it is that his eye ranks second or third among the paths to his brain. It is just as simple and sensible as that.

The same principle applies to writing in a language such as French, German, or Italian. It applies to a specimen of writing in Chinese, Japanese, Persian, Arabic, Hindu, or Greek, but you would have to know the alphabet of that particular tongue well enough to know what visual details (such as *i*-dots, *t*-crosses, umlauts, or accent marks) were required.

If you are asking someone to write a few sentences for you to analyze, you must be very careful *how* you phrase your instructions. If you show him a paragraph and say "Copy this" or "Write it just as it is" or "Write exactly what it says," then you may be telling him to pay greater attention to details than he normally would do. Even persons who are not eye-minded *can* put in all the details if they are specifically directed to do it.

Meminisse juvat. Prodana
Nevesta- dolce far niente.
Non abbiamo bisogno
di niente.

3-6 Latin and Italian phrases by eye-minded ex-seminary student.

My method is this: I give the person a pad each page of which has a sentence printed across the top in boldfaced letters, a half-inch high:

Write: Handwriting tells 2,458 details!

I say: "Here is a sentence that has four words and a number. Will you please write it as naturally as you can, starting with this word first," (and I point to the appropriate words as I talk) "then these two words, then the number and the last word." I am careful not to pronounce any of these four words, because I want him to *read* them for himself.

Sometimes the client himself or someone else in the party will say: "You mean *copy* that sentence?" or "You mean you want me to write it exactly as it is?" To get around this without letting him know what I am looking for, I say: "No, if you copied it you would have to *print* it. I want it in your natural handwriting, just as you normally would do it." Even then someone in the group may read it aloud to him, including punctuation or spelling, or may remind him that he forgot the colon or the exclamation point. If so, I interrupt by saying: "Now, now, let him write it his way. Here's a pad so you can write the sentence the way you do it."

It took me many years to develop the sentence that I use, one that gives me so much information in so few words. You will note that it contains two capital letters and two words that start with small letters. It has two unusual marks of punctuation, the colon and the exclamation point. It requires four *i*-dots and four *t*-bars. It contains a long word (eleven letters) and two that are frequently misspelled, "write" and "details."

In addition to the sentence, I ask the person to sign his name the way he would normally put it on a check, and I later inspect this for visual details, such as *i*-dots, *t*-bars, and especially periods after initials or after such abbreviations as "Mr." or "Jr."

Obviously, if a person writes all of this with no mistake at all, he must be visual-minded. Occasionally some other trait, such as coordination, will be so strongly indicated that it must be considered equal in importance to his sight. But this chapter is not concerned with these relatively rare and borderline cases; its purpose is to show you how you can learn, by looking at a sample of writing, whether the writer is primarily eye-minded.

Some persons get all the details into the writing but place them somewhat carelessly. Others put each *i*-dot precisely over the point of the *i;* each *t*-bar is exactly two-thirds of the way up the stem of the *t,* with half the bar on each side of it; and the colon, the comma, and the exclamation point all rest just on the line of writing and are properly spaced in relation to the words, although the pad has no ruled lines to guide them. Persons so meticulous tend to be perfectionists.

Write: Handwriting tells
2,458 details.

3-7 Chemical engineer, meteorologist for huge airline, absentmindedly omitted exclamation point.

A minor variation of the eye-minded individual is one who does put in all the other visual details, but fails to cross a *t* or leaves off the exclamation point. This indicates absentmindedness. The accuracy of detail in the rest of the writing proves the writer intended to put in the details omitted, but simply forgot.

In summary then: if a person's writing shows attention to all visual details, including punctuation and spelling, he is eye-minded; the more of such details he omits, misplaces, or changes from the original copy, the more this indicates that sight is *not* the primary path to his brain.

Chapter 4. Are You Ear-Minded?

The term "ear-minded," as used in this chapter, does not refer to a person's hearing in a strictly physical sense. You can wear a hearing aid and still be ear-minded in the sense that I use this phrase. For instance, Beethoven was ear-minded long after he became so deaf that he could not hear himself play the piano; although deaf, he could still think in terms of sound and he continued to compose music.

Suppose you are right-handed but you broke your right arm or mangled your right hand in an accident; you would remain right-handed. As soon after the injury as you could grasp a pen or pencil, you would prefer to use that hand for writing. You may have been born with only 25 percent of normal hearing or as you grow older you may lose 50 percent or more of your originally normal hearing, but neither of these facts prevents your being an ear-minded person if you were born one.

Now if you do fit into this classification, you probably have a good memory for voices you hear on the telephone. Or if you are fond of jazz, then hearing a few bars of a popular song or just humming it to yourself will be enough for you to recall the precise words that fit those bars. Or it may be the other way around: whispering or humming a few words of a popular song may help you to recall the actual notes well enough to play them on any instrument for which you have skill. If such is the case, you will always hear the song in your mind as if it were being sung and not as if you were reading the words aloud from a printed page. If you forget a line or two, you also will have forgotten the corresponding music, but as you begin to recall the missing phrases they will bring back the correct notes, or vice versa.

Ear-minded people frequently spell poorly in English. The language has many words with silent letters, many words that sound alike but are spelled differently, and others that are spelled alike but are pronounced differently. Such persons tend to spell words phonetically, but in English this is frequently misspelling.

Dear Hal: I hope Rudolph makes his first stop at your house each Christmas

Johnny Marks

4-1 Composer turned publisher; author of *Rudolph the Red-Nosed Reindeer;* note long *t*-bars.

Originally I had thought that in a language where words were literally phonetic, such as Spanish or Italian, spelling would be much easier for ear-minded people, especially if the language were their native tongue. However, during my first year in Mexico, I frequently heard an idiom that meant "It does not matter" or "It is not important." When I asked my cook, who had finished four grades of elementary school, to write the phrase for me one day when I heard her use it, she wrote *No liase.* I searched in vain through two Spanish-English dictionaries and one huge dictionary that was entirely Spanish for a verb that could possibly have a form like *liase.* Months later I learned from a schoolteacher that my cook had been trying to write the first three words of a more complete phrase: *No le hace nada,* which means literally "To you it makes nothing." So you see you can have difficulty even with a phonetic language if you spell by ear.

Now look at the specimen of your writing that you prepared

4-2 Professional bass fiddler.

according to the instructions in chapter 2. There is a tendency for ear-minded people to misspell each of the words in this short sentence and they sometimes transpose one or more of the figures. Did you put *White* or *Whrite* or *Wright* for the first word? Did you omit the *d* in *Hand?* Did you put a double *t* in writing or leave out the *w* or spell it *wrighting?* Did you write *telles* or perhaps *tills?* Did you put *detailes* or *detales* for the last word? If you made any such errors, you are probably ear-minded; each is one of the common mistakes an ear-minded person makes in writing this very simple sentence. Such a person is likely to omit any or all the marks of punctuation—colon, comma, and exclamation point—and to use a lower case *h* on *Hand;* but it is unlikely that he would put capitals at the beginning of *tells* and *details,* as the action-minded people do. The ear-minded person usually makes abnormally long *t*-bars; the *t* occurs four times in the sentence, so at least two or three times it would have a crossbar longer than the vertical height of the *t*-stem. Occasionally the ear-minded person writes a 3 in place of the 8 or the 5.

Once a gentleman from Canada put in his specimen both *Wright* and *Handwrighting.* The way he wrote the figures (a 4 with a triangle

4-3 Misspelling by ear-minded engineer-inventor; Canadian.

in its top, and an 8 made with circles) indicated that he was an engineer. From the gaps in the pencil line, the originality in his capitals, and the marked forward slant, I knew he was highly creative. Putting these two facts together, I decided that he was probably an inventor rather than an artist, a writer, or a composer. His signature told me he could be the owner or manager of a company.

I told him he should be engaged in creative development and research work in a field that concerned machines producing sound, such as telephones, phonographs, tape recorders, or dictating devices; that he had an inventive mind that had undoubtedly produced one or more patentable products; and that he should be "head man" in a company, preferably one that he himself owned. And finally, from certain peculiarities in the shapes of his *w* and *n,* I told him that he had learned to write in a country that was under the British flag.

When I had completed my analysis, the gentleman said: "Professor, you amaze me. I have always considered handwriting analysis on a par with tea-leaf reading and phony astrology, but you've been right on every single point. I am a native of Canada and a graduate engineer. In fact, I have earned seven college degrees in chemistry, electronics, and mechanical engineering. I am an inventor. I hold seventeen patents on a device that is in the field of sound, a dictation machine that competes with several made in the United States. Some

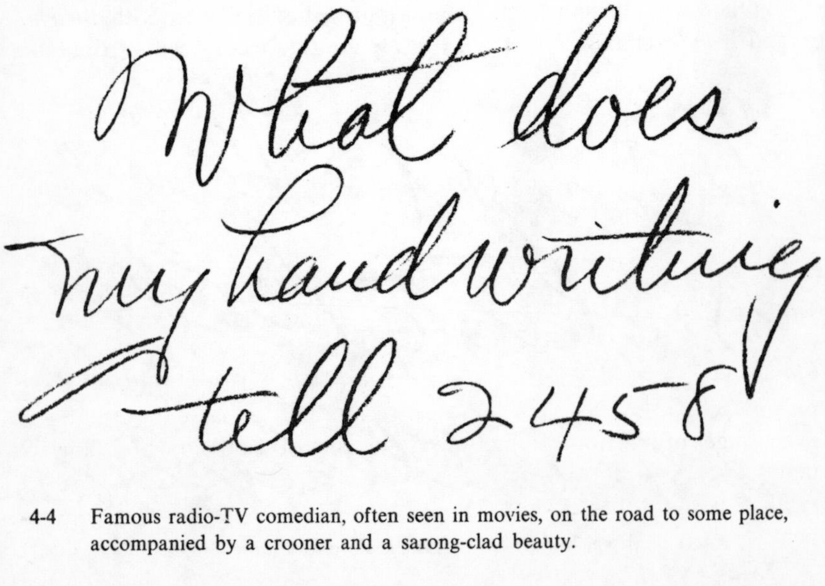

4-4 Famous radio-TV comedian, often seen in movies, on the road to some place, accompanied by a crooner and a sarong-clad beauty.

years ago I organized a corporation to manufacture and sell the machine, and I am both general manager and chief stockholder in the company. But how did you get all this information from a signature and one sentence?"

This man had also written extremely long *t*-bars, as most ear-minded (the term "auditory-minded" is synonymous) people do. I cannot tell you why this is true; I only know that having analyzed the writing of literally thousands of persons who make a living in the field of sound—musicians, disc jockeys, lecturers, radio and television engineers and performers—at least 90 percent of these persons do make noticeably long crossbars on the letter *t* in their normal writing. Scientific information obtained by this kind of observation is called empirical data. Such observed data, properly recorded, is the basis for medicine, anatomy, geography, geology, chemistry, and many other sciences.

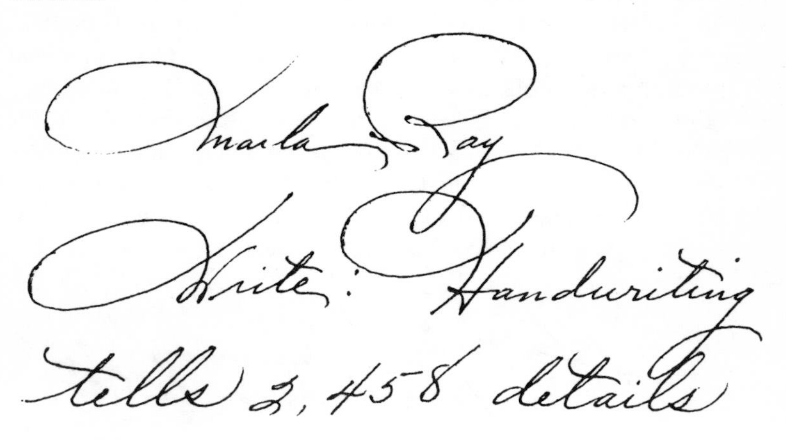

4-5 Actress who has also recorded many fairy tales and stories in various languages for children; note talent for visual accuracy.

Now eye-minded people tend to observe small details, so their writing is frequently small (that is, short in vertical height of the letters), with *t*-bars only half as long as the *t*-stem is tall, this being the correct size according to the penmanship texts. Auditory-minded persons tend to write somewhat larger scripts and to make their *t*-bars even longer proportionately in order to be able to see them easily. The major exception to this general rule is, understandably, the ear-minded person whose secondary talent is an almost equal visual perception.

WRITE: Handwriting
tells 2,458 details!

4-6 Printing by visual-minded woman.

If you are an auditory type, you can now understand why you may have made a lower score on an intelligence test than some friend or relative who is really less intelligent than you. Such a test is usually presented in printed form; eye-minded people absorb every detail of the wording and therefore start out with accurate information for solving the problems given. But the ear-minded person easily overlooks detail; thus in preparing your answer you make a mistake not because of lack of intelligence but because of faulty visual observation of the terms stated. Because the instructions on the test were prepared by visual-minded professors (if they were not visual-minded, they probably would not have become teachers in the first place), the problems are full of details that only eye-minded individuals can absorb readily. I consider that ear-minded and action-minded students are handicapped by at least ten to twenty points on an I.Q. test as compared with their visual-minded classmates.

Handwriting tells
2,458 details

4-7 Radio announcer who now has his own TV show.

Now suppose your writing does indicate that you are an ear-minded person, what good is this information? In the first place, you would realize that you should not attempt to make your living in an occupation that requires careful attention to visual detail, such as bookkeeping, stenography, law, library work, school teaching. For you, such work would be as awkward and frustrating as writing exclusively with your left hand if you were normally right-handed (or vice versa).

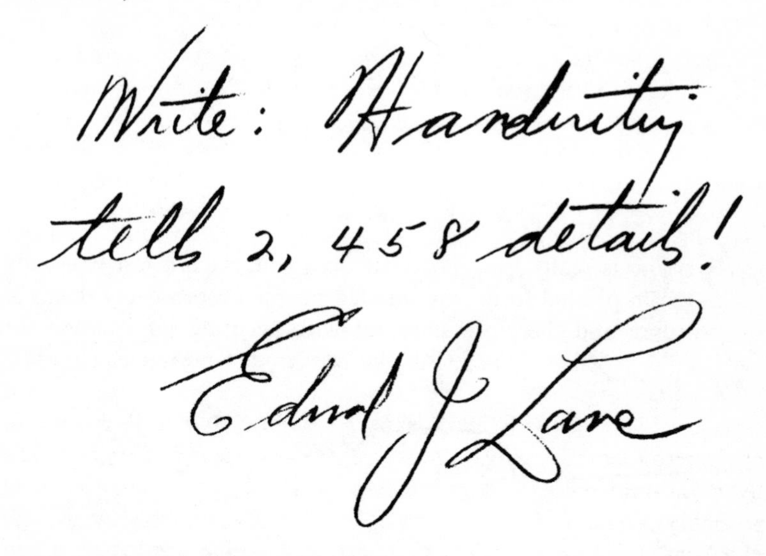

4-8 Leader of an orchestra that often replaces Guy Lombardo at the Roosevelt Grill; calls himself "detailist."

However, you would fit naturally into one of the many fields where sound is a major element. These fields range from telephone operator to grand opera. They include all phases of performance in music and radio; the engineers and technicians who make, service, or operate tape recorders, radios, television, telephones, and dictation machines;

Write:
Handwriting tells
2,458 details!

4-9 Composer; author of eighteen texts on music; now producing audio-visual aids to music education.

and the military men in the sonar and signal corps. Many actors and dramatic coaches are ear-minded as are lecturers, teachers of public speaking, and of course composers and songwriters.

I have analyzed the writing of journalists who were ear-minded, whose talents were used in interviewing people and remembering what was heard. I have encountered creativity in persons who wanted to become professional writers but who found that the physical labor of putting black marks on paper by any known method of pen, pencil, or typewriter was simply too laborious. When these people started using a machine for dictation, they found they were able to get their thoughts on paper in salable form.

Write Hand-
writing tells
2453 details —

4-10 Retired grand opera singer.

My experience indicates that every person who is ear-minded is per se a potential musician who should learn to play at least one instrument and should continue to play that instrument as a hobby if not as a profession. However, I have found many ear-minded people who think they are unable to play any musical instrument because they have never had any training and have never had the patience to pick out a tune for themselves on an instrument such as a piano or a guitar.

Write Handwriting
tells 2 458 details

4-11 Pianist, originally in dance orchestra; plays dinner music only.

Recently I told a young woman that she had an extremely sharp ear for pitch discrimination (a good "musical ear") and that she should be successful as a performer in some field of music. She and her husband laughed loudly at my statements; at the end of my analysis I found out why.

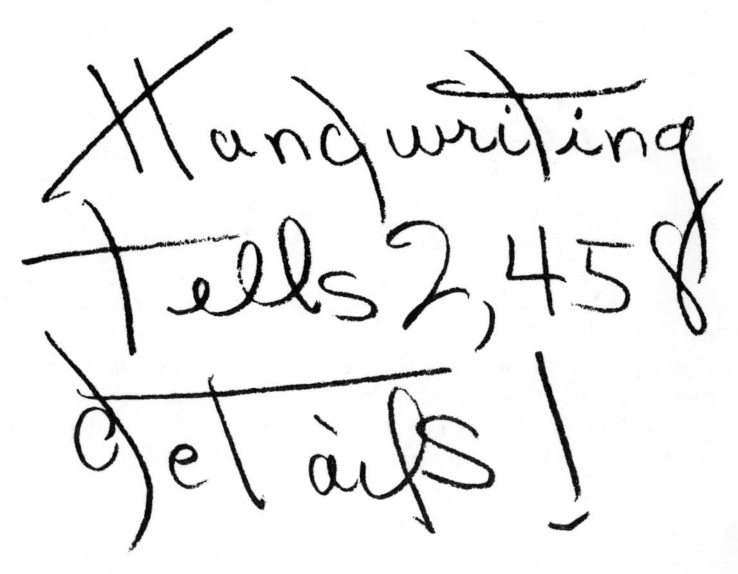

4-12 Singer-artist-writer who should use dictating machine for writing.

The lady told me that she had a notoriously poor ear for music although all her brothers and sisters and her mother and father were good musicians. When she was two or three years old, it seems, she tried to sing along with a phonograph that was playing and was so far off key that her older brothers and sisters made fun of her. They assured her she couldn't carry a tune in a bucket, as they put it, and she had better not try any form of music. My opinion is that this ridicule prevented her from developing what I considered her obvious musical talent.

In actuality, this woman works as a professional lecturer and dramatic coach; she is especially noted for her ability to teach actors and actresses how to use dialect in their performances. She was very good at imitating a Scotch burr or an Irish brogue and even taught professionals how to perfect them for stage roles. I insisted that her ear for pitch must be as good as her ear for dialect. I think she would have been just as good in music as in public speaking and dramatics

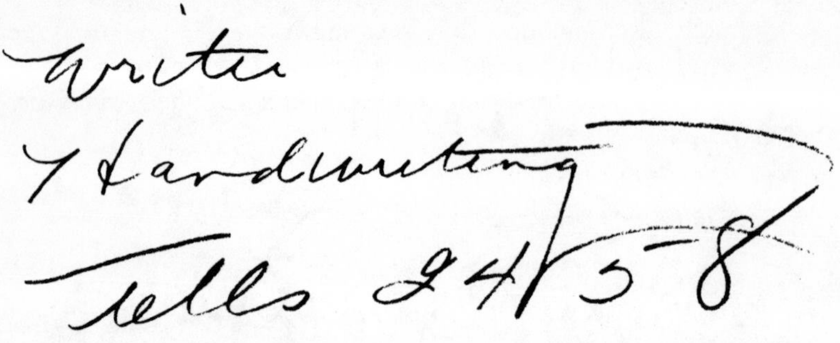

4-13 Illustrates musical ear of drama coach who "can't carry a tune."

had she not been so ridiculed at an early age by her older brothers and sisters.

If you are ear-minded, another interesting field open to you is that of interpreter (as distinguished from translator) of one or more foreign languages. You would need to learn languages by the oral method, preferably in a school, city, or country where they are spoken and before you reach your twenty-first birthday, if possible. If you learn a language after the age of twenty-one, you are likely always to have a noticeable accent; but the better your perception of pitch, the more readily you can eliminate this by practice. If you possess the somewhat rare combination of an exceptionally good ear plus exceptionally good control of the muscles in your larynx, then you can probably learn to be fluent in a foreign language without any trace of an accent even if you are well beyond voting age when you first begin to learn it.

Another field in which ear-minded people are frequently successful is that of specialty selling or any form of selling to an audience, such as an auction or the kind of demonstrations that the pitchmen use on the boardwalk at Coney Island and Atlantic City. However, most successful salesmen whose writing I have analyzed are actually action types, though they may have a very good ear as a secondary qualification. In some instances these talents are reversed: a successful salesman may be an ear-minded individual with a strong action talent as his secondary qualification.

If you are a personnel director, knowing whether a specific applicant is ear-minded can be extremely important to you. You would obviously not want to put him into a position where a great deal of visual accuracy is required, but you might have in your organization a job that would fit his particular talents perfectly.

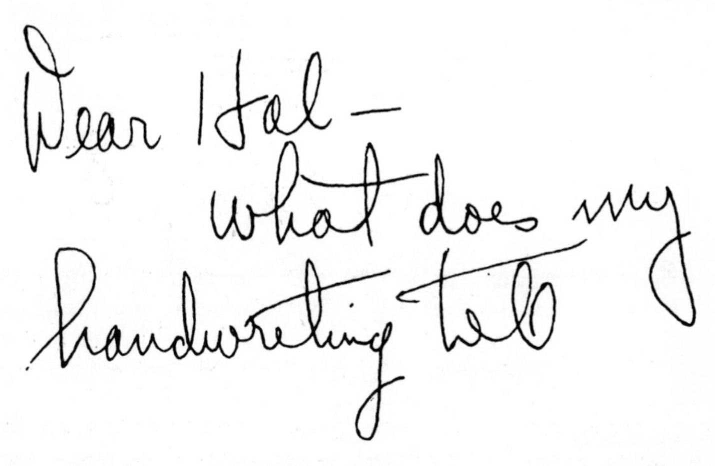

Dear Hal—
what does my
handwriting tell

4-14 Radio singer turned salesman; could be a good auctioneer demonstrator.

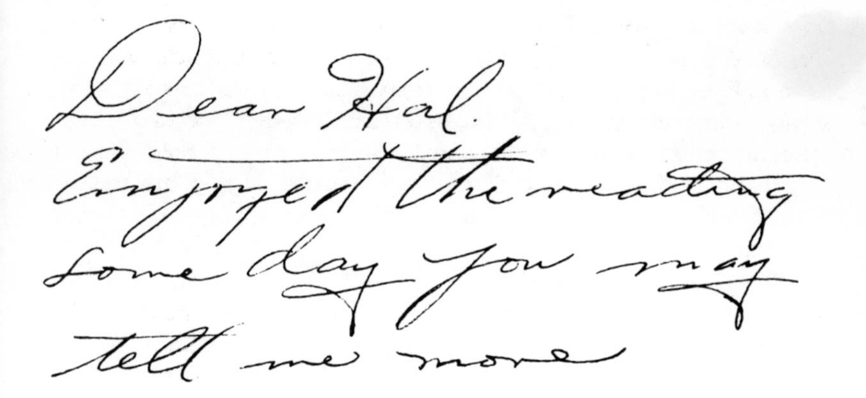

Dear Hal.
Enjoyed the reading
Some day you may
tell me more

4-15 Ex-trombonist of symphony orchestra, became salesman, now vice-president for sales of a big corporation.

Chapter 5. Are You Action-Minded?

It has been estimated that only 10 percent of the population of the United States are action-minded individuals or, if you prefer the scientific term, "kinaesthetic types." This figure compares with 60 percent who are eye-minded and 30 percent who are ear-minded. So if you are an action type, you are a relatively unusual person in that only one out of ten persons fit into this class.

Note:
Handwriting tells
2,458 details!

5-1 Power, speed, hearing; clerk who built up big printing company he owns.

Three major characteristics can be distinguished in action: power, speed, and accuracy. Every football team must contain men who show these three characteristics. Every offensive squad contains a fullback who is powerful enough to bull his way through a wall of opposing linemen and gain a precious one, two, or three yards for a first down or a touchdown, even if he has to drag six tacklers along with him to make that yardage. Such a player is usually the biggest man on the team in physical bulk and weight and frequently in his performance bracket as well.

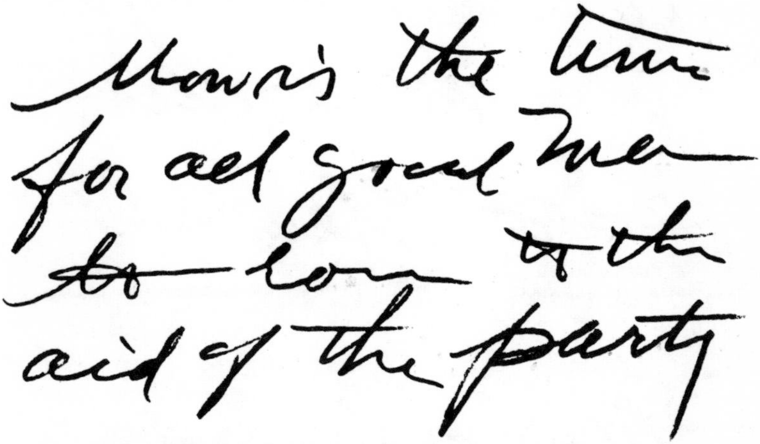

5-2 Speed; ex-district attorney, now general counsel and member of board of one of our largest corporations.

At the opposite end of the scale was little Albie Booth, the famous All-American from Yale, who is reputed to have been able to run 100 yards in ten seconds wearing his full football uniform, although he was so slight they say he only weighed 150 pounds in a heavy rain. Since the track record for the hundred at the time he was playing was only about four-tenths of a second less than this, it is probable he could have broken that record had he preferred track to football. Few coaches can find men of this caliber, but every team needs a half-dozen men noted for their speed in order to get under a punt or a forward pass or to overtake an opponent running with the ball.

And in these days when the game takes to the air, every coach looks for a player who can develop the astonishing accuracy in forward passing of a Y. A. Tittle. The drop kick has been out of style for years, but every team needs a man who can punt accurately or kick for that extra point after a touchdown. And an educated toe that can produce a field goal from as far back as the twenty-five- or thirty- or thirty-five-yard line has won many a game in the past few years. Players who have the accuracy necessary for these feats must possess an extraordinary degree of coordination and could use that coordination equally well in many other fields, such as the putt in golf, the serve in tennis, or the competition of rifle shooting.

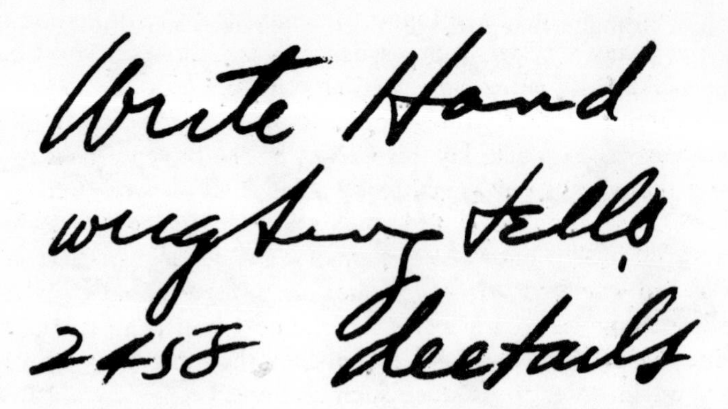

5-3 Hearing, power, coordination, speed; eye surgeon, former football star noted for drop kick, passing.

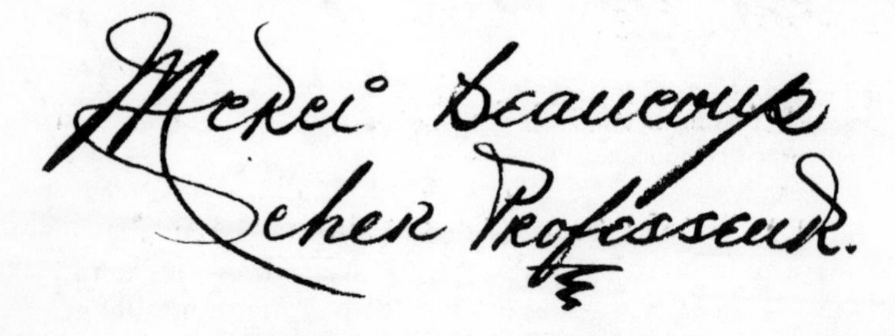

5-4 Coordination, artistic curves, noticeable in foreign language.

Is coordination your major talent and, if so, how much of it do you have? This is almost the easiest thing to tell by handwriting, and certainly it is the easiest to demonstrate to a person who knows nothing about graphology and has never had his script analyzed before.

What does
my handwriting tell?

5-5 Coordination shown in printing.

If the writing or printing look as if they might have been done by a penmanship teacher, then the writer obviously is very well coordinated.

The simplest way I have found to demonstrate coordination to a skeptic is to use a paper napkin which has a scalloped edge (I carry such a napkin with me as part of my equipment). Now if you brought me this sample of your writing and it showed the characteristics I'm about to discuss, I would lay this napkin on the table in front of you and run the point of my pencil along its edge as if I were tracing the curves of its scallops. I would say to you: "If I ask you to draw me a line and put in that line curves as smooth and regular as these in the napkin, you would have to have a great deal of coordination to make each curve a precise duplicate of the one next to it. And if you draw this line rapidly, you would have to make a rhythmic movement with your hand in order to produce such scallops."

Write:
Handwriting tells
2,458 details!

5-6 Dancer pianist; she's got *rhythm.*

Then I would take my card and lay it over the word *tells* in your handwriting sample in such a way that the edge of the card was parallel to the line of writing and left exposed just the bottom one-third of each letter. I would show you that the lines connecting each letter with the one that follows it form a series of curves which tend to be almost as smooth as the scallops on the napkin even though they are much smaller, and I would say that obviously you would have to move your hand in a precise rhythmic coordinated movement in order to produce these scallops.

If you were well coordinated, I would use the card to cover up in a similar manner the top two-thirds of *Write* and then *details* to show you similar scallops in the base of these words. You may have written the two *n*'s in the word *Handwriting* as if they were *u*'s; in such a case the base line of *Hand* and of *riting* in the word *writing* might easily show similar scallops. I would also point out similar curves in your signature if they were there.

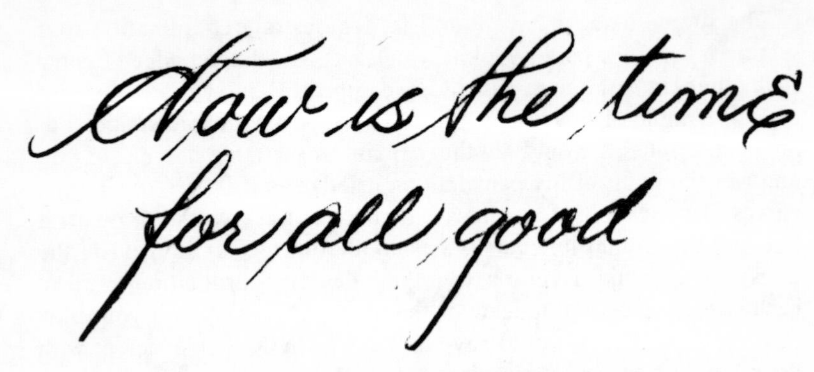

5-7 Coordination, power, speed; advertising manager—skates, skis, types, plays piano; has won several rifle-shooting championships.

Thus, the number and evenness of such curves in your writing demonstrate how coordinated you are. The more coordination you have the more likely it is that this is your major talent or at least that, of the three action characteristics, it is your best. If coordination is one of your strongest characteristics, you should be able to learn quickly and perform well any movement that requires rhythm: dancing, ice skating, skiing, water skiing; the Australian crawl, the breast stroke, and the flutter kick in swimming. This coordination is not limited to movements of your feet; you should have an aptitude for learning finger movements, such as typing or piano playing. In general, the smaller the scallops in your writing are, the more likely you are to possess the digital dexterity of a typist or a pianist; the larger the scallops, the more likely you are to excel in movements of the arms and the legs, such as swimming, dancing, and ice skating. Among artists, those who show the small scallops usually do well in miniatures, sketching, or water coloring. Artists painting in oils on an easel normally use an arm movement rather than a wrist or fingers movement; an aptitude for such arm movement is shown in handwriting by the larger size of the scallops.

If your writing shows relatively small but accurate scallops, you possess the manipulative dexterity to learn to operate any kind of office machine: stenotype, comptometer, keypunch, computer, duplicator; in fact, if you are that well coordinated you can probably learn to operate any kind of machine that interests you, from a jeep to a helicopter.

If you are interested in music, a marked rhythm in your writing would indicate that you might do well to stick to a rhythm instrument such as drums, vibraphone, or piano. Of the two major phases of music—rhythm and melody—a trap drummer, a bongo drummer, or a cymbalist needs to have only rhythm. A piano player in a dance combo may not need much more sense of melody (pitch discrimination) than the drummer, but a pianist in a symphony orchestra and a concert pianist need as much of a sense of melody as a good violinist. The handwriting of the concert pianist would therefore show that he was an ear-minded person with a very strong talent for digital dexterity; the pianist in the dance combo would be more likely to show action as his major talent with coordination as his primary aptitude and a sense of pitch as second or third among his list of talents. You can see why it is important to learn not only all of the talents shown by a person's handwriting but also how to rank these talents in the order of their importance.

Write : Handwriting
tells 2 458 details!

5-8 Young French lady, pianist.

Now coordination is also the talent that produces accuracy in the field of sports. Perhaps it strikes you as odd that I would describe people so different as an expert typist, a dance band pianist, a figure skater, and a sharpshooter each as an action-minded person with coordination as his major talent, but such is the case. Indeed, I would go so far as to say that any person who is really a champion in any one of these fields could learn to be adept in any one of the others if he would spend enough time in learning and in practice.

Write: Handwriting
tells 2,458 details!

5-9 Power, speed, coordination, sight, hearing; sales manager of New York City's biggest new hotel.

Now let us consider a different action trait: power. In this discussion the word "power" does not refer only to physical strength; the concept includes energy, drive, willpower, and competitive spirit. "Power" includes whatever it is that would make a little 90-pound blonde, age sixteen, run away from home to join a vaudeville troupe and spend years of hardship and hunger and hours and hours of practice in carrying out her firm determination to become a star adagio dancer.

Handwriting tells
2,458 details!

5-10 Power, sight, speed, coordination; resident manager of big hotel; note indications of German education, in *H, t* and *2.*

Power in this sense of go-getter spirit—"The guy has guts!" is another way of putting it—correlates almost precisely with the amount of pressure shown in handwriting. In analyzing a specimen of handwriting I consider the pressure in grades running from zero to ten: #10 pressure is that which is necessary to make ten carbon copies; #5 pressure makes five copies, and #0 pressure, no copies at all.

Dear Hal,
What does my
handwriting tell you?

5-11 Rhythm and power; small adult dancer, specializing in tap, adagio.

More explicitly, when the writing is done on the first page of a pad of 16-pound bond paper with a sharp #1 pencil, #5 pressure will make such indentations in the second page of the pad that it must be thrown away because it is unsuitable for future specimens; #10 pressure will make the third page similarly unusable. Anything beyond #10 pressure indicates such an extreme that the writer may well be so torn by inner conflicts that he will be unsuitable for normal occupation, or he may be a mental patient.

In order to demonstrate the amount of pressure to a client, I carry with me when I am working a penlight with two fresh batteries in it. I turn the page of writing face down in front of the writer and put the flashlight at the left-hand edge of the page so that its rays slant horizontally across the back of the paper. The ridges caused by the pencil marks are easily visible under these circumstances, especially in a semidarkened room or in a shadow cast by the room's brighter lights. In writing with #0 pressure, it is impossible to tell from the slanted rays of the penlight that there is any writing on the other side at all. When the pressure is #1 or #2, usually only the downstrokes of the pencil marks will cast a slight shadow. If the pressure is #5 or heavier, you can run your fingertips over the back of the page and feel the ridges. I have never analyzed the writing of a person who was successful in any field that involved selling—advertising, merchandising, sales promotion, fund raising, publicity, or public relations—whose writing did not show at least #5 pressure. Those who were really outstanding in their field had pressure of at least #8.

5-12 Speed, power, hearing; attorney adept in jury trials and politics.

Among professional men I find that engineers seem to write with the heaviest pressure; physicians in general seem to write with more pressure than do C.P.A.'s and other accountants; and these men in turn seem to write with more pressure than lawyers, college professors, and writers. Among attorneys however, those with the heaviest pressure seem to go in for jury-trial law or politics or both, and seem to be the "salesmen" in the field of law. Lawyers with more sedentary interests, such as those who compile textbooks or write treatises on the theory of law, show a great deal of intelligence, logic, and sheer brain power in their handwriting, but very little pressure.

Most of the men whose writing shows pressure ♯5 or heavier have been successful on school teams while they were growing up; this means their forcefulness of personality was manifesting itself as competitive spirit. The few exceptions to this were mostly farm boys who devoted their efforts to fishing, hunting or horseback riding, which used up their energy but were not as competitive as team sports.

I recall an experiment I made when I was a graduate student grading papers for an English professor. When about 150 freshmen whom I had never seen before turned in to me their first themes of the semester, I separated the papers into four stacks. In one pile I put those whose writing showed the heaviest pressure; in the second pile, the writing with medium pressure; then a pile of papers with relatively light pressure; and finally a stack that showed relatively little or no pressure at all. Then I checked the high school records of these students to find out in which activities they had been successful.

The students with the heaviest pressure all showed success in competition. They had been team captains or they had been successful in winning letters on high school teams in two, three, or even four different sports. Almost every man whose writing was in the stack with medium-heavy pressure had won a letter for participation on at least one team, but he was rarely an outstanding player. The students whose writing was in the light-pressure stack had achieved success in lesser activities; some of them had held class offices or had participated in some of the clubs or perhaps had been the president of a history club or something of that sort. And of course those whose writing had almost no pressure had had almost no extracurricular activities while in high school.

I was surprised by the fact that almost the heaviest writing among the whole collection of papers was from a man whose record showed that he had not won any award on any team, but he had won out over thirty applicants in a big city high school for the position of manager of the football team. He had also been president of the senior class and captain of the debating team. I made a point of looking him over when I called the roll in the next class and then I understood: he was a little runt barely five feet fall who weighed scarcely 100 pounds; he couldn't possibly have made a football team in those days of brawny players. But some twenty years later I did learn—this time without surprise—that this man had become an outstanding jury-trial lawyer and a very powerful politician. In his state he was called "The

King-Maker"; without his approval no politician could be elected to statewide office.

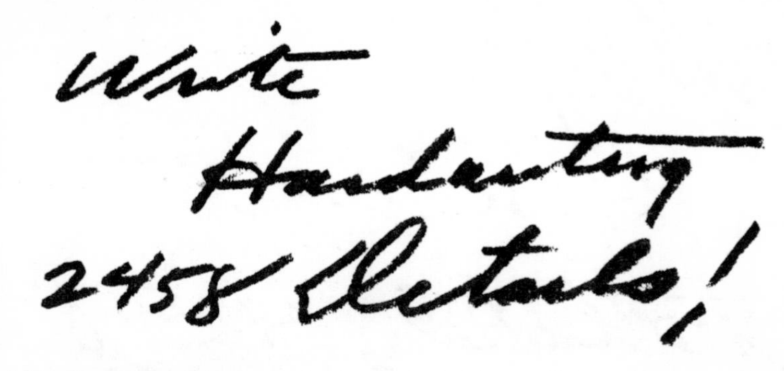

5-13 Small man with extraordinary power, speed; started by trading in used cars; now owner of big corporation.

The term that psychologists apply to what I here call "power" is forcefulness of personality. Those who have studied this trait say that it is not one you are born with; and if you acquire it at all, you usually do so before your sixth birthday. "Power" is not exclusively the possession of the male sex; many women acquire it also. Among the thousands of women whose writing I have analyzed, those who held positions of major importance in a business enterprise—such as merchandisers, managers, or buyers in big department stores; owners of beauty shops or blouse shops; or heads of departments in banks or insurance companies—all showed noticeable forcefulness in their writing, usually at least #5 pressure or heavier.

I have found that almost everyone without training in handwriting analysis is sure he can tell a woman's writing from a man's simply by the way it looks. If the writing is fairly large, dashing, and heavy, he will call it masculine; if it is light, precise, small, and especially if it slants backhand, he will say it is feminine. In my opinion such characterization is completely false despite the fact that there are a few professional graphologists who do claim that they can tell the difference between a man's writing and a woman's.

There is another theory I have read in some books on graphology which states that the heavier the writing the more extroverted the writer and that writing with little or no pressure is always the mark of an introvert. I am in complete disagreement with this theory and in chapter 8 I will tell you why.

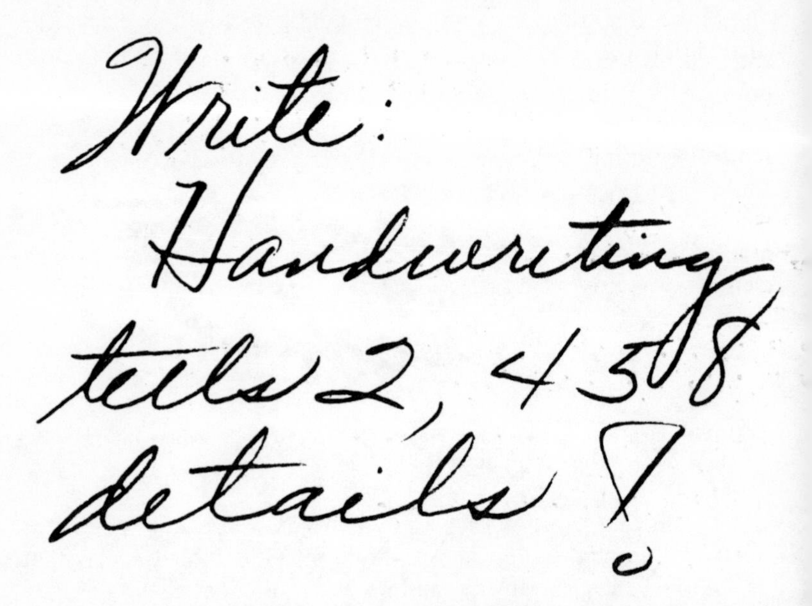

5-14 Power, speed, coordination, sight, hearing; beauty operator, now owns big company making and selling her products to hair stylists.

Forcefulness of personality shows itself in many ways; a person possessing it is said to have drive, enthusiasm, aggressiveness, competitive spirit, resistance, guts, go-getter spirit, and even stubbornness. I know of no personality or aptitude test that gives any clue as to the existence of forcefulness and none that makes any attempt to measure it. Yet it is the trait that personnel directors desire most in a prospective employee and at the same time it is the one least easily determined by a personal interview with the applicant. It is considered even more important than high intelligence, since personnel directors and college administrators alike agree that just average intelligence together with dogged persistence are more likely to produce successful achievement in any endeavor than very superior intelligence (as shown by I.Q. tests) coupled with laziness.

Any personnel director who will read and apply the next paragraph, however, will have an instant and accurate test that can become more and more helpful to him as he becomes experienced in using it. All he needs to do is to give an applicant a pad of 16-pound bond paper and a #1 pencil with a sharp point. Let the person write anything he wishes, such as his name, address, and a sentence or two, on the top page of the pad. The director can then turn the page over and run his fingers across the back of it to see if he can feel ridges produced by the pencil in writing. If he cannot feel any ridges or cannot see them as indentations in the second page, then he should remember this: if the writer does not wear a lot of lead off the pencil while writing, then he certainly has too much lead in his shoes, and he will never be active enough to make you glad you hired him. So tell him good-bye now—right now—unless you need him only as a file clerk or a second assistant bookkeeper.

5-15 Speed; well-known actress.

Furthermore, if the personnel director in making the above test watches the movement of the hand during the course of the writing, he can easily tell if it is moving at a fast, medium, or relatively slow rate of speed. Although the speed of the writing is easy to calculate when you watch it, an accurate estimate of this speed is one of the most difficult things to determine if you do not actually see the writing being done. Dr. Robert Saudek, a graphologist whose books I have studied with admiration, has worked out with great care and research a set of tables for determining speed in writing and has formulated more than two dozen rules for obtaining an accurate estimate. If you really need to use such scientific exactness, I refer you to Dr. Saudek's book, *Experiments with Handwriting.*

One of the simplest indications of writing speed is: in slow writing the *i*-dots are usually dots and the *t*-bars are long narrow *quadrangles;* the faster the writing, the more the *i*-dots and the *t*-bars tend to become long narrow triangles pointing toward the right margin.

5-16 Note left-handed *t;* singer turned writer and lecturer.

Incidentally, if the point of a *t*-bar is toward the left margin of the page, then the writing was done with the left hand. Whether a left-hander writes with his hand above or below the line of script, about three out of four will make the *t*-bar with a motion from right to left, whereas every right-hander makes it from left to right. The direction of the motion is always from the blunt end to the pointed end of the bar. The popular notion that all left-handed writing is backhanded and that all backhand writing was done by the left hand is, under ordinary circumstances, completely false according to my observation.

If you find in a given sample of writing a few very light lines that are not intended to be part of any letter but that run from the end of a word toward another word or back toward a *t* that needs to be crossed, these marks also indicate that the writing was done at high speed—the writer did not even have time to lift his pencil completely from the paper in moving toward the next letter. Sometimes parts of letters will be omitted, such as the beginning upstroke of the loop on an *h* or a *b* or the entire upper loop of an *f,* or the return loop on the bottom half of the *f.* Saudek says any person trying to disguise his own script or imitate the script of another will always write much more slowly than his normal speed.

But now let's get back to our original question: how can you tell from looking at a handwriting specimen if the writer is action-minded? The simplest way of course is to determine whether he is either eye-minded or ear-minded according to the principles in the previous chapters of this book. If he does not fit into either of these classes, then you can assume that he is action-minded.

Certain other characteristics will help you. Most action-minded people cross *t*'s but frequently omit all or most of the *i*-dots. They tend to substitute dashes for marks of punctuation, such as a colon or an exclamation point. In the sentence: "Write: Handwriting tells 2,458 details!" they nearly always capitalize the first word of the sentence

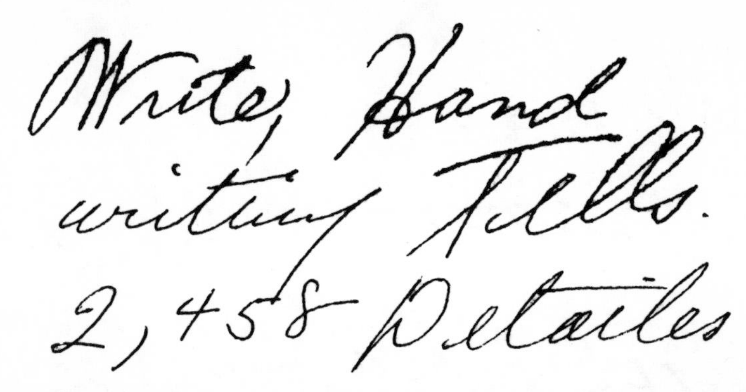

5-17 Power, speed, hearing; sales manager of machinery company, started as mechanical engineer.

but frequently write a small letter for the *H* in "Handwriting" and capitalize the first letters of *tells* and *details.* Most of the time action-minded persons do get the numbers correct, although they sometimes substitute a space for the comma or leave it out entirely; occasionally they will write a 3 instead of the 5 or the 8.

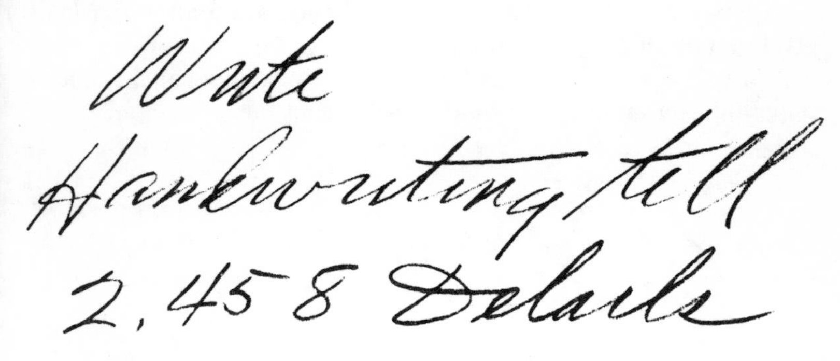

5-18 Power, speed, hearing; says he had "no schooling" but now owns and runs five companies he started.

Let me stress again that being action-minded is not necessarily correlated with physical health or strength. The great majority of eye-minded people use their eyes so much that they must wear glasses as they grow older, but they still think and remember in terms of vision. Likewise, an action-minded person may lose an arm or a leg or become so afflicted that he is confined to a wheelchair or rocking chair, yet he still remains an action-minded person.

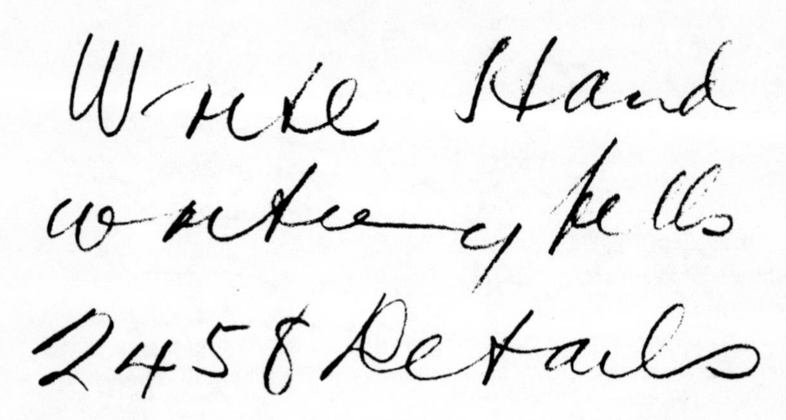

5-19 Power, rhythm, speed; singer, songwriter, composer, voice coach who "taught Sinatra proper breathing."

There is an old American adage that implies that anybody can do anything if he only has the persistence to work hard at it and to practice it enough. In other words, if you really want to be the world's champion rifle shot, even better than Annie Oakley, you buy a good rifle plus several thousand rounds of ammunition and you go and practice faithfully: bang, bang, bang, bang. First you win a local match, then a state championship, followed by a national championship, and you are well on your way to being the world's greatest.

5-20 Coordination, hearing, sight, power; artistic flourishes; former grand opera prima donna who swims, dances, sketches, plays piano well.

Here I tell you flatly: it just isn't so. How long would it take you to teach a blind man to paint portraits? If you think this is an exaggerated example then how long would it take you to teach a color-blind person to make a copy of a painting by Corot or Botticelli? Even a person who has only a part of this defect, a person who is blind to red and green but not to blue and yellow, will have lifelong difficulties with traffic lights, no matter how hard he tries.

Often you will read or hear such statements as these: "Any schoolboy can learn to spell if he will just study"; "Anybody can be a good salesman if he tries hard enough"; "Anybody who can walk can learn to dance well"; "Anybody can play a chord organ or a guitar, learn to swim, make out his income tax report, play golf, play bridge, learn to shoot straight . . . ."

Again I say, no matter what they tell you, it just isn't so.

Unless you were born with a great deal of coordination, enough for it to show in your writing as your major talent, you might wear out a dozen guns and burn up a million rounds of ammunition in practicing, and you would still never be good enough to win even a county championship, much less a statewide rifle match.

Study the principles in this book. Learn from your writing precisely what your major talents are and how they rank in importance. Then stick steadfastly to those occupations and hobbies that use these talents. In this way, your work and your play will come easily for you and you will excel in what you do.

Let your own analysis of your own writing tell you: are you eye-minded, ear-minded, or action-minded?

Chapter 6. Does Your Handwriting Limp?

Suppose you see a stranger walking down the street, and you notice that whenever he takes a step with his right foot he moves it in an awkward manner; in other words, he is limping. Now you don't have to be a physician to realize that if he limps, there must be something wrong. The defect could be something as simple and temporary as a tack in his shoe, a wrinkle in his sock, or a blister on his heel; or it might be something permanent and quite serious. But if the man limps, there is *something* wrong.

You can draw two further conclusions from watching this stranger's limp: first, the defect is below the waistline and, second, it is on the right side of the body. Obviously an injury just above the waist, such as a broken arm or dislocated shoulder, or one on the left side, such as a stiffened left knee, would not cause him to limp on the right foot.

Just as the foot makes a limp in the action of walking, so does the hand make a limp in the action of writing, and for the same reason: a defect in the body of the writer. The kind of limp in handwriting almost anyone would notice is one caused by a sprain or injury to the writing hand itself, such as a broken finger or wrist. From long experience and hundreds of examples I have seen, I assure you there are characteristic limps in writing that indicate defects, injuries, pain, or illness in other parts of the body. Sometimes I have found indications pointing to a defect the writer was not yet aware of or denied vigorously, but the correctness of the handwriting analysis was confirmed by later events. Sometimes you will need a magnifying glass to find the limp in a script, but once you have seen it, it will be quite unmistakable, and you will be able to find it a dozen times on every page.

In this chapter I will discuss how to recognize a limp in the writing when you see it, how to judge by the location of the limp in a letter just what portion of the body is affected, and the several possible causes for the various limps.

First, what is a limp in writing and how do you recognize it?

There are abnormalities of movement that are caused by habit and not by any physical defect. You may have seen, for example, "the rolling gait of an old salt," the result of a sailor's habit of bracing himself to meet the unexpected shift of a ship at sea. Every police officer learns to recognize the shuffling steps of a man released after a year or more in a chain gang; the ex-prisoner will very often walk hesitantly for the rest of his life, as if still feeling the weight of the chains that once joined him to the other men.

Similarly in writing we find such habit formations as the engineer's four and eight (48), the accountant's two, four, and five (2455), the British two and four (24), and the continental European one and seven (17) all of which are written differently from figures used by other people in the United States.

The word "limp," however, as applied to either walking or writing, refers to a defect or injury, not a peculiarity such as those mentioned above. In this chapter the word "limp" as applied to writing means a point or angle in a line that should be a smooth curve; a curve that is convex when it should normally be concave (or vice versa); a gap in a line that should be unbroken; an abnormally thick or thin spot in the width of a line; or a marked variation in pressure, from heavy to light to heavy and so on. Each of these limps is illustrated later in the chapter by copies of actual handwriting samples taken from among the thousands in my files.

Now, if there is a limp, how can you tell in what part of the body the defect is located? To learn the correlation of the parts of the letters with parts of the body, look at the diagram on page 66. Notice that the right and left sides of the body are indicated as in a mirror, not as in a picture.

With tiny arrows I have marked the limps in the handwriting specimens on the following pages. In some cases the defects are enlarged or exaggerated so you will not have to use a magnifying glass as I did on the originals. These illustrations do not include any that show sex appeal or sex abnormality; these will be discussed with examples in chapter 10.

I assure you that each of the following stories is an actual, true case history taken from my files, though I have had to change a few minor details to avoid identifying some individuals and to maintain their privacy.

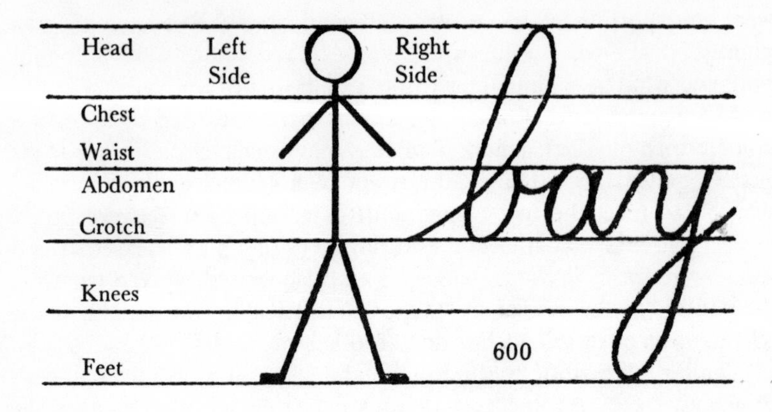

One evening I was invited to join a table of three men, all strangers to me, in a big hotel where I was giving a continuous series of lectures on graphology. I did not know it at the time, but they had previously agreed among themselves that my analyses were based on snatches of conversation I heard in a group, so they had decided to make no comments on what I said and to answer no questions I might ask. Far from hindering me, this was a great help. It enabled me to concentrate exclusively on the writing, without interruptions.

As usual, I gave each man a pad and pencil and asked him for a signature, and then told him to write the words in the sentence: "Write: Handwriting tells 2,458 details!" which was printed across the top of the page. By getting all three samples first, I avoided the possibility that the writing of one man might be affected by something I had said in analyzing one of the others. I was also able to compare the size, the pressure, and the detail or lack of detail in one sample as compared with these characteristics in the other two.

From the form of the signatures and the style of writing, I suggested that two of the men would be suitable for practicing law and the third for some phase of journalism or publicity.

This last man wrote the word *details* with a tiny bump on the right side of the letter *t*. I pointed this out and told him I interpreted it to mean that he had an illness, an injury, a wound, or a pain, located in the right-hand side of his abdomen, near the waistline. I suggested such possibilities as a war wound or chronic appendicitis, and told him that, since I was not a physician, he should consult his doctor if he were not already aware of the trouble. After I had completely finished all three analyses, this third man told me: "Professor, you were accurate in everything you said about each of us, except on one point. I have never had a wound, an accident, or an operation. I do not have chronic appendicitis. I have not been sick a single day in the past ten years. I have regular medical checkups and last month I had a complete physical examination, and I'm about the healthiest specimen in this entire room. Why I put that little bump in the letter I have no idea, but it certainly has nothing to do with my health."

Details

6-1

In the face of this emphatic denial, I could only apologize for my error and explain that no system of dealing with the human personality is infallible, including graphology, just as there is no system of medical diagnosis that is infallible.

I later became quite well acquainted with these men and, during the time I stayed at that hotel, they often brought in their friends and associates for writing analyses. About six months after I had met them, one of the two attorneys came to me and said: "Hal, do you remember the day you analyzed Bud and Johnny and me, and you told Johnny he had an illness or pain in the abdomen?" He was referring to the man I had called a journalist, who was actually an ex-reporter turned publicity director for a political party. I assured him I remembered both the analysis and the flat denial of its accuracy.

"Well, Johnny sends you his regards," the attorney said. "He is in Wilson Hospital and recovering nicely from his operation. Yesterday morning he was operated on for a slipped disc in his spine, on the right-hand side at the waistline, exactly where you said it was. . . Your analysis was so accurate it frightened both of us. We were in the midst of a big, important campaign, and Johnny simply could not take time out for an operation at that time. Only his wife, his doctor, and I knew about it, but he was sleeping on a board and wearing a back support all day, yet he was still in almost constant pain because of that slipped disc."

Of course, an injury such as a slipped disc may be shown in an entirely different manner. Figure 6-2 shows the specimen of a man who owns a factory in Brazil, where he lives. He told me he suffered

6-2

from a slipped disc on the left side, just below the waist. While analyzing his handwriting, I had noticed the indentation in the bulb of the *d* of *details* and marked it with a small arrow, as you see. If you drew a line across the tops of the *e, a, i,* and *s,* this line would correlate with the waistline of the body, according to the diagram I gave you earlier. This man's defect is below that level and on the left side of the letter. So I was able to point out to him the indication that he had some pain or injury and to tell him its approximate location. I was not able to tell him that it was a slipped disc; so far as I know, kidney or colonic or other abdominal trouble might cause a similar irregularity in the script.

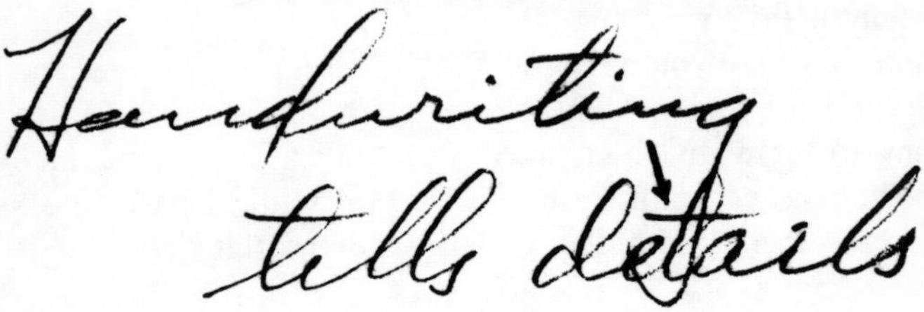

6-3

Figure 6-3 contains the writing of another man who had suffered the same injury in the same location, although his physician called it a "ruptured disc." It was caused by a fall at age seventeen, about a dozen years before this sample was written. Note the point where an abrupt swerve occurs in the downstroke of the letter *t;* observe that it is on the left side of the letter, at or below a line that would connect the tops of the *e* and *a*, representing the waist. The doctor had told this man that it was just below the waist, on the left side of the spine. This parallels the first example above; in both cases the subconscious mind of the writer uses the letter *t* as a symbolic representation of the human spine.

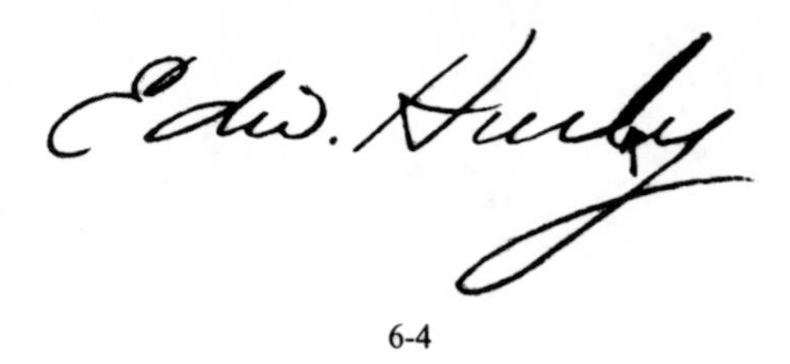

6-4

In Figure 6-4 the letter *l* represents the spine, and the slipped disc is somewhat below the waist on the right side (see arrow). In this man's case the injury was severe enough to put an end to his career as a professional dancer and force him to learn another profession.

One of the firms for which I act as consultant is a large and successful advertising and public relations agency. The owner of the business sent me a specimen of the writing of an executive in a big company that is one of his clients. The specimen was written on a sheet from a memo pad; the page carried no printing or typing, so there was no title, no letterhead, nothing to indicate the company name. The signature was completely illegible, so there was no way I could have located or traced the man, even had I wished to do so. Unable to decipher his name, I called him "Mr. W.H.M." in my written analysis, although I learned later these were not his initials.

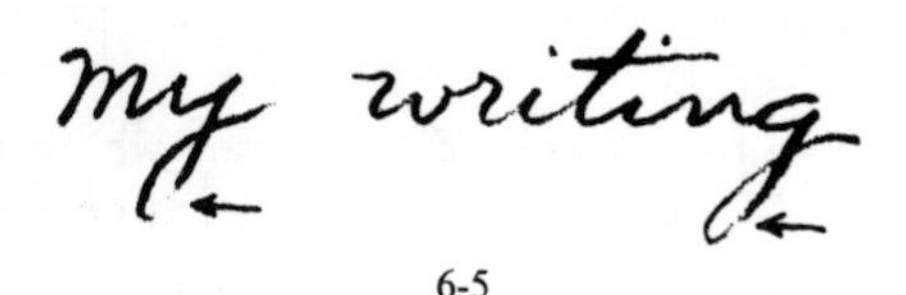

6-5

In examining the memo under a powerful magnifying glass, I discovered that many of the *g*'s and *y*'s had a thin spot in the line at the bottom of the right side of the lower loop. In my analysis I said: ". . . now shows some physical disability affecting the right leg, probably near the ankle—perhaps a football injury or a war wound."

This man was the personnel director for a very large manufacturing company. Weeks later I visited his office to discuss some business matters with him and I noticed that he walked with a distinct limp; his right leg ended in a hoof foot (*pes equinus*).

Figure 6-6 was written for me by a guest staying at the Statler Hilton Hotel in New York, where I have been lecturing for the past several years. I observed that he had a clubfoot on the right leg, so I

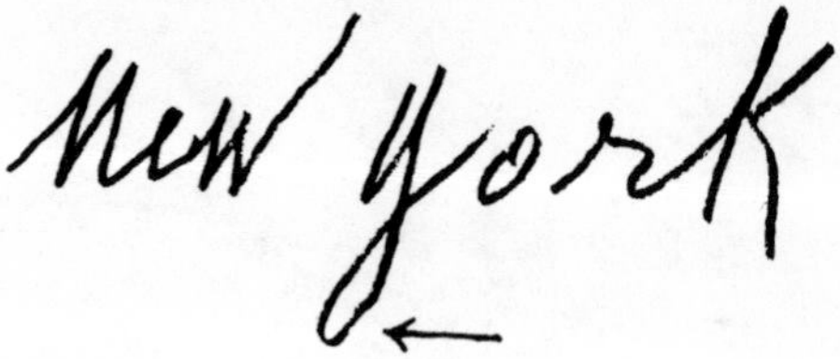

6-6

asked him for a specimen of his writing for my autograph collection. He did not understand any English, so first I tried Spanish, but he answered me in Italian. I was able to put together enough words in his native tongue to persuade him to write in it a translation of the English sentence printed on the pad, but when I looked at it, there was no indication of his handicap. He refused to write his name, but finally wrote me another sentence of his own choosing. This time the *Y* in *New York* gave me exactly what I was expecting, so I marked it with the arrow you see in this copy.

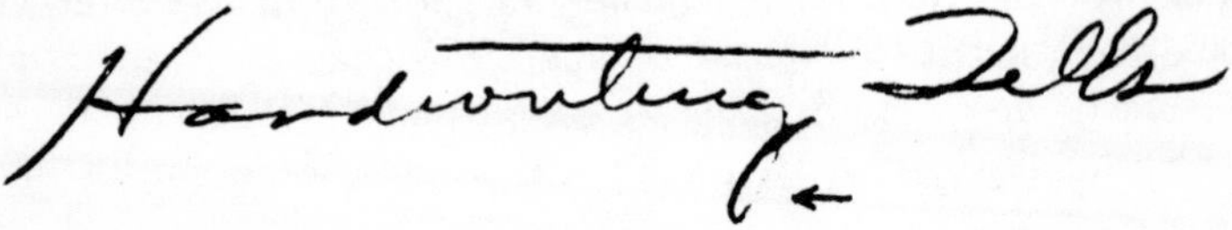

6-7

Figure 6-7 shows the writing of a veteran whose right leg was amputated above the knee as a result of a wound received during the battle of Iwo Jima. He gets about so well that few of his customers are aware of his injury; he owns and operates successfully a business that sells desks and other office supplies and equipment. The arrow points to the very light line that makes the right leg of the *g* in *Handwriting,* which you can readily compare with the normal heavy one on the left.

The woman whose handwriting is shown in Figure 6-8 had an operation on her right leg and hip—"just like the one Arthur Godfrey had"—about five years before she wrote this sample. As a result, she not only walks with a limp that gives her pain in her right calf, but also suffers pain in the muscles just above the hip. The most noticeable indication of all this is the dent in the tail of the *g* at the point that corresponds to the calf of the right leg, but there are also indications, which I have marked, that correlate with the pains in the waist on the right side. Observe that in the *y* of her name, the

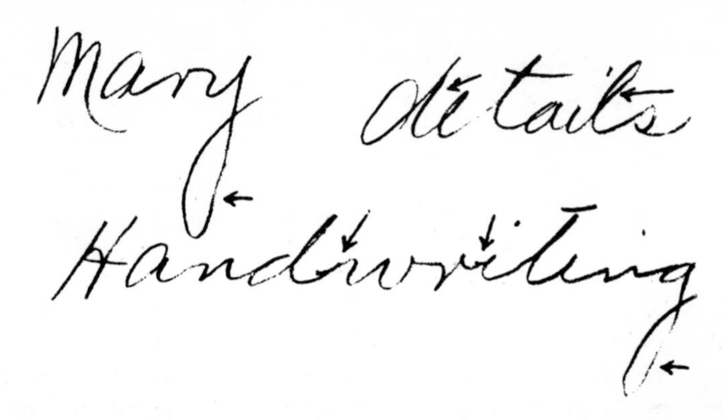

6-8

downstroke makes an angle to the left just a trifle below the point that would correspond to the right knee, but it is so slight I doubt if I would have noticed it had I not first seen the indentation in the *g*. Because of the operation, she told me, she had had to give up a successful catering business that she had built up for herself and take a less tiring job as a dietician.

6-9

The case illustrated in Figure 6-9 is somewhat similar, except that the injury to the hip and to the spine just above the waist, both on the right side, were caused by an automobile. The accident happened about eighteen months before I analyzed this woman's script, and she was still using a cane to assist her walking.

If a man were born with both feet deformed, you might well expect from the above examples that the bottom of the letter *g* in his writing would show defects on both sides; in Figure 6-10 you have just such a specimen. At the very bottom of the downstroke the line suddenly becomes so thin you can hardly see it; then it veers sharply left in a straight line instead of a curve and makes an abrupt angle into another very thin spot that corresponds to the location of the left foot. I have marked these with arrows, but you may need a magnifying glass to verify my description.

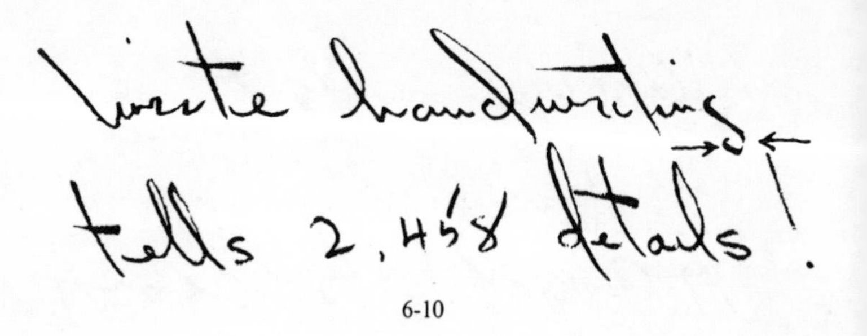

6-10

If a man let such a handicap make him a permanent invalid, it would be understandable; but not this one—he's an activist. The omission of the colon and two *i*-dots proves he is not eye-minded. The speed and the ♯8 pressure indicate he is probably an action-type; and you will remember I told you such people frequently use a small letter where my sentence has a capital, just as he did. The gaps in the writing line and the backhand slant indicate dramatic creativity, as will be discussed in a later chapter. By means of special braces on each leg, plus a crutch and a cane, this man gets around well enough to run his own publicity and public relations business successfully. His initials are so big and so unique in shape that I could not read his name; the signature is just what you would expect from a man in his business.

6-11

All of the above examples show pains or defects that were present at the time the writing was done. The handwriting in Figure 6-11 indicates the subconsicous can carry a scar for years. The woman who wrote this now has a grown daughter of her own, but when she herself was a child of three, she grabbed at a pot of soup boiling on her mother's stove and spilled it down her left leg, and she still has a big scar as a result. She described the scar as extending from three to six inches above the knee.

In analyzing this woman's writing I had mentioned that she probably had suffered an injury or wound that affected the left knee or an area somewhat above it, basing my opinion on the sudden thinning of the line in the upstroke of the *g*, which is marked with a small arrow. She was astonished that such a thing would show in her writing, but she confirmed my interpretation by telling me about her childhood accident. She has two similar letters in her name; one shows the same defect as this *g*, but it is not so pronounced, and the other carries no such indication at all.

In contrast to the handwriting shown in Figures 6-1 to 6-11, which reveal permanent scars or defects, the next specimen shows a temporary one. With a magnifying glass I spotted the angle in the *g* of *writing;* I asked my client to write the word *singing* so I would have two more *g*'s to look at. This time there was an unusual thickness of the line, precisely at the bottom of the left (upward) stroke. When I marked these details with arrows and explained that I thought they meant a pain or injury in the left foot, she said: "Why, I just noticed it myself today! Yesterday I was having a little pain in the bottom of my left foot, but I thought it was just a wrinkle in my stocking or a grain of sand in my shoe. It hurt a little this morning, and when I looked at my foot I found a thick spot, like a corn, right in the ball of my foot, and it was sore when I pressed on it. I told my husband I'd have a doctor look at it as soon as we get back to Buffalo. But just imagine your finding something like that in my writing!"

6-12

This woman called it a corn, but from her description I assume her chiropodist would call it a plantar wart. It seems significant that what she called "a thick spot" on her foot would show as a thick spot in her writing, and you can see for yourself that it does. This spot occurs in two of the five *g*'s she wrote, including one in her signature. (Figure 6-12)

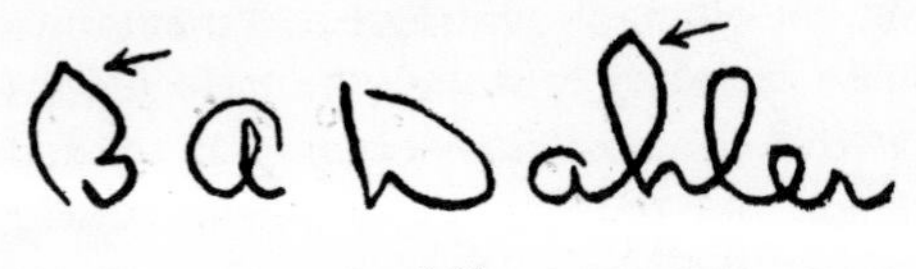

6-13

I have in my files the autograph of a man who says he is quite deaf in both ears, but I made a memo on the back of it that he wears a hearing aid always in his right ear. This gives sufficient reason for the fact that the limp in his writing occurs only on the right side of the letters: it is his *right* ear that is "on his mind." There is no known explanation for why the defect shows in only one of his three initials and also in the *h* but not in the *l* of his name, or why it appears in several other upper-loop letters in his writing but not in all of them. (Figure 6-13)

6-14

However, this situation prevails in most specimens of handwriting that reveal a limp—the irregularity occurs only occasionally and not in every word. For example, the publicity director whose handwriting is shown in Figure 6-1 wrote for me four words containing *t,* but only a single letter in the entire sample, including his signature, showed the bump in the illustration.

Figure 6-14 shows the variation of pressure I found in the handwriting of a woman who is a partner in operating a chain of ladies' wear stores in Arkansas. In this case, every word she wrote, including her signature, showed this unusual irregularity of pressure.

I have seen this type of limp thousands of times; it usually is found in the writing of a person whose energy comes in jerks rather than an even flow. Such a person gets fatigued much more quickly than is normal and needs many rest periods while working—say, five minutes of rest every hour on the hour or, as a substitute, a twenty- to thirty-minute siesta every three or four hours.

The four most frequent causes of this faltering energy, in order of their frequency are: (*a*) low thyroid activity, (*b*) low blood pressure, (*c*) low blood count (or other blood defects, such as pernicious anemia or leukemia), (*d*) low blood sugar (this is the opposite of diabetes). Many persons suffer from the first three conditions at the same time; it is possible that the subthyroid activity lowers the blood pressure and the blood count.

I picked the example in Figure 6-14 from among dozens in my files because none of the above causes apply to it and the writer flatly denied that she had any illness whatsoever. She said she hadn't been ill in years; she worked long hours every day and never got tired; she had never felt better in her life.

Six months later her husband, back in New York on a buying trip, told me that two weeks after they had arrived home from their last trip she was hospitalized for hepatitis, and she was still so weak and tired she couldn't come along with him on this trip. A letter he had just received from her showed the irregular pressure I had originally pointed out. This is only one of many instances I have found where the writer's subconscious mind has put into the script indications of facts of which he was not consciously aware.

6-15

Figure 6-15 shows the writing of a woman who had anemia. The line that forms the last letter of each word is thin, light, and droopy, as if her hand were so fatigued it barely had enough strength to complete the word. I have marked these with arrows, along with one or two similarly weak letters. Excessive fatigue at the end of a day or, especially, periods of exhaustion that occur too frequently or after too little exertion to be normal are symptoms of anemia, low blood pressure, or both.

Figure 6-16 contains the writing of a woman whose physician said she had low blood pressure; notice the recurring light spots in the middle of the words. There is no significance in the difference between this writing and that of Figure 6-15. Both kinds of defects in

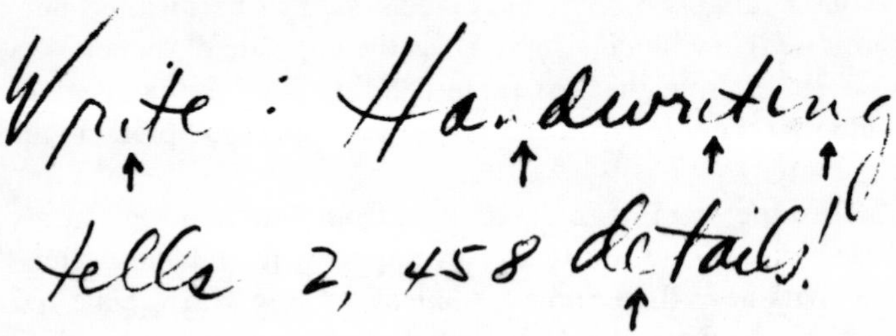

6-16

the script indicate frequent periods of weakness or fatigue, and there are many conditions that can cause such weakness, for instance a subthyroid condition, leukemia, etc.

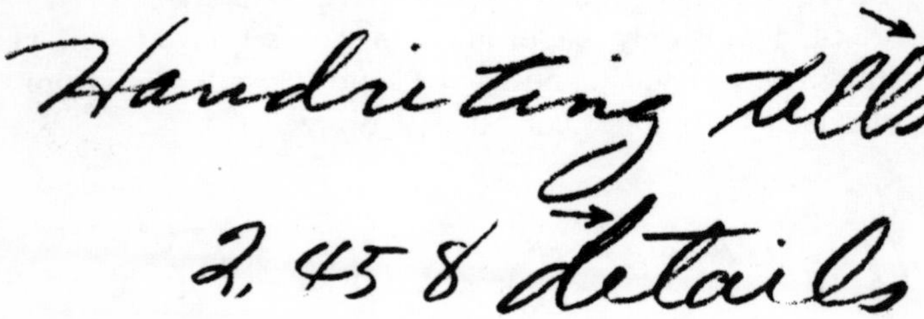

6-17

In Figure 6-17 we have two quite different limps in a single specimen, but both happen to be on the left side. This specimen was written by a divorcée (notice the *g*) who was in an automobile accident some years ago. She suffered a big gash in her scalp above her left ear, but the long scar it left is effectively concealed by her hair, so she was surprised when I marked the *l* in *tells* and the *d* in *details* and explained that they meant pain or injury on the left side. I was somewhat confused myself, because the first limp seemed to imply a head injury and the second, a somewhat lower area, such as the arm or shoulder. She cleared up the difficulty by explaining that for some weeks she had been suffering from rheumatism in her left arm, with pains so severe that it was hard for her to do the typing required in her job as secretary.

The awkwardness of this next specimen is caused partly by the fact that it was written left-handed by a person who is right-handed. The writer is an ex-Army nurse who was wounded while working under

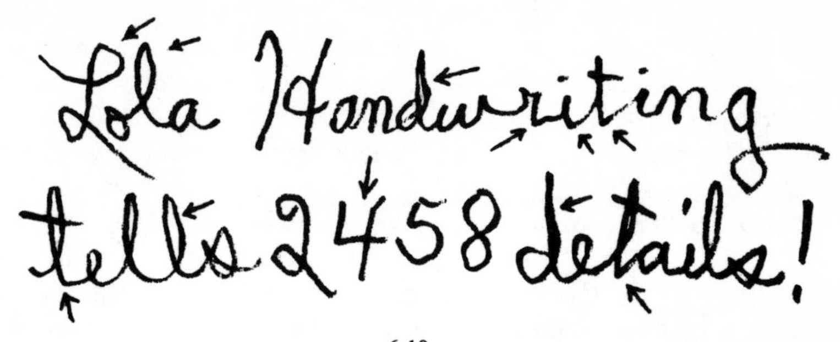

6-18

fire with our troops, shortly before the fall of Bataan; she lost the use of her right arm, although it was not amputated. Numbers rarely show evidence of such defects, but here I have marked the 4 because of the angle at the top of what would normally be a straight downstroke; the arrows indicate similar abnormalities in her name and twice in the letter *d.* When I pointed out these details to her in making the analysis, she told me briefly about her war injury. (Figure 6-18)

She also confirmed that she is a widow (note the way she wrote the *g*). I have also marked some sharp angles in the base line that indicate she has had some illness or injury near the crotch, perhaps a miscarriage that required later surgery, or a hemorrhoidectomy, or a hysterectomy.

Write: Handwriting
tells details!

6-19

A stammer and a stutter are somewhat different when you hear them, but they are similar in that both represent a kind of muscular spasm that forces repetition of sounds; both are the result of a mental or emotional condition rather than some physical defect in the muscle themselves.

Figure 6-19 shows the writing of a man who stutters; he has suffered from this malady as far back as he can remember. There is not as much evidence of stuttering in his handwriting as I would have expected, but note the one place where he repeats a line that was quite satisfactory originally, and one letter in his signature contains a similar repetition. The base lines of the *a* and *i* in *details* also contain unexpected angles that may have resulted from muscular spasms in his hand similar to the spasms in the mouth muscles that cause him to stutter.

Figure 6-20 is a specimen of a man who stammers, "... but not too bad," as he told me. Note the repetitions and irregularities caused by spastic action of the muscles; many of these irregularities are in locations that correspond with the head. This man's real name is not "Paul Rand." I have drawn this diagram to show you how his initials also indicate some difficulty in or near the left side of the head. The odd thin spots in Figure 8, which he wrote, are caused by spasmodic variation in the pressure used in writing.

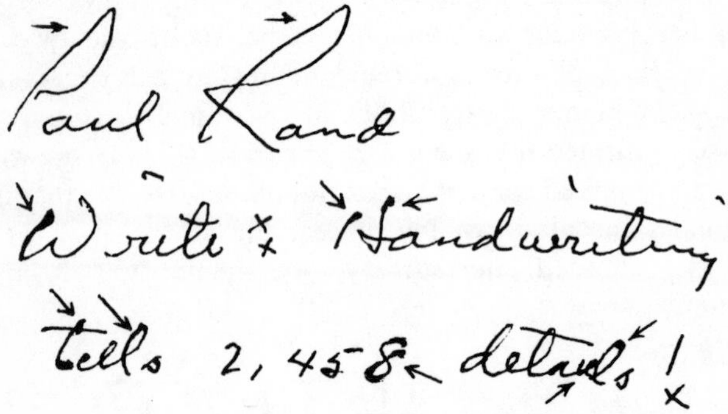

6-20

It must be that all the troubles these limps indicate have grown worse since his retirement or have been intensified by a slight stroke that he did not tell me about. The tiny *x* he uses instead of a period indicates that he was a reporter for several years (he confirmed this fact), but he was in the Army long enough to retire as a brigadier, so the stammer he has had all his life was apparently not bad enough to hinder his military career. When I met this man he was actively engaged in running a real estate business he had established. While his script shows he suffers from one or more difficulties, its ♯10 pressure indicates the drive that has enabled him to succeed in spite of these troubles.

Figure 6-21 shows the writing of a man who has undergone six surgical operations in the past eighteen months; it is not surprising

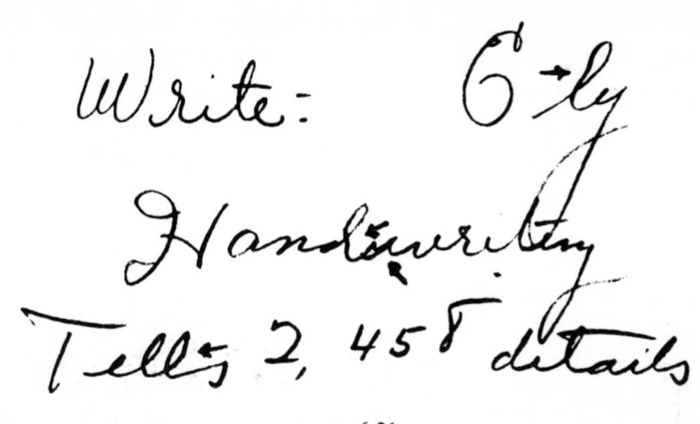

6-21

that he is so weak his writing has almost no pressure at all. The operation that has worried him most, apparently, was for the removal of a cancerous tumor on the left side of the abdomen at the waistline. The defect he made in writing the *w* was so obvious even to him that he tried to correct it by rewriting part of the letter, but the defect on the left side of the second *l* in *tells* and the same part of the *l* in his name escaped his notice. The *Ely* illustrated here is a copy of part of his name, the rest of which has been deleted to conceal his identity. The location of the irregularities cited corresponds to the abdomen and the waist.

6-22

Now we come to the consideration of heart trouble—the physical kind, that is; the romantic kind will be discussed later. The sample in Figure 6-22 was written by a woman almost two years after she had a heart attack, which hospitalized her for a month and was characterized by severe pains in her right shoulder and arm. The letter *l* in *gelatin* has a defect I have marked with a small arrow; as you might expect, it is on the right side of the letter, but a trifle low, almost at a point that would correspond to the waistline. You will note that it makes a tiny *v* inside the *l*.

The indication of heart trouble that I have found most often is an angle in what would normally be a smooth curve, or an unexpected thin or weak spot in a line, both of which are illustrated in Figure 6-23.

6-23

Figure 6-23 shows the handwriting of the same woman as above, written about two and a half years after the sample in Figure 6-22 and about six months before she died of a heart attack. Again I have marked with arrows the points for you to study. The *b* and *l* have thin spots; the *k* of *Thanks* and the *t* of *want* and of *etc* all show an angle, and in each case the defect is on the right side at a location that correlates with the chest.

This brings out another point I want to make: approximately half of the indications for heart trouble I have seen were on the right side of the letter. In this particular case my friend told me that she had felt severe pains in the right arm, so that may be the explanation in other cases also. My theory is that defects on the right side of the letter mean that the writer's trouble is on the right-hand side of the heart itself.

Because heart attacks and strokes are so common among older people, I am showing you here a specimen from a woman who had had both. As you can see, the writing is part of a thank-you note written four days after Christmas and therefore approximately two months after the coronary spasm she mentions. Most of the defects you see here are caused by the stroke. The repeated wavering lines in the left half of the letters *b, h, k,* and *l* suggest that it is the left side of

I have been sick since the 9th of Oct. had a slight stroke got better + then had a coronary spasm + was put back to bed + am up + down now. We have all had a nice Christmas.

6-24

her body that is most affected. However, notice the *l* in *all;* the sharp angle in its right half indicates the heart trouble. (Figure 6-24)

Figure 6-25 shows parts of the addresses of two envelopes, written approximately a year apart, by the same woman. The first and larger

Mr. + Mrs. Hal Falcon

Mr. + Mrs. Hal Falcon

6-25

one was written about six months after she had her first stroke, and I have marked with arrows its indications—all on the left side of various letters. Notice how the writing on the second envelope (which carried the message about the coronary spasm pictured above) shows precisely the same defects in the same locations of the same letters! In addition, this time there are other limps: an angle in the *l* at a point that correlates with the heart, and similar corners in the *o* and *n,* all of which would seem to indicate that the "9th of October . . . slight stroke" had caused difficulties on the right half of the body, apparently near the hip, that were not experienced after the first stroke.

Irregularities in handwriting due to paralytic strokes are so often seen that I want to give you two additional samples, without much

Glad to have your schedule
& we both hope you all have
a perfectly swell trip, vacation,

6-26

comment, since the defects are so obvious. The second was written with the left hand by a seventy-year-old attorney, originally left-handed, whose left side was so badly crippled by his attack that he had to write with his right hand for about a year. He said that he had gone back to writing with his left hand about a month before he gave me this specimen. (Figure 6-27)

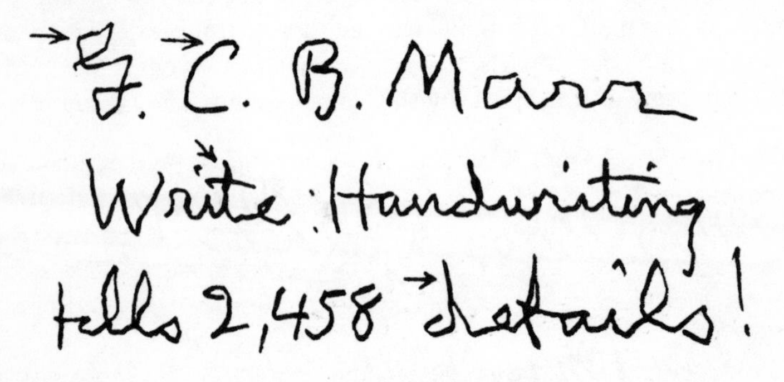

6-27

Arthritis is another crippler whose traces can be seen in handwriting. The word shown in Figure 6-28 was written by a lawyer to tell me the trait he considered his worst fault. All the joints of his fingers and knuckles were swollen to more than double their normal size, each one marked with a hard lump he said was caused by arthritis.

Impatience

6-28

The resulting awkwardness is apparent in his script, which is quite different from the stroke specimens above.

The handwriting in Figure 6-29 shows one of the graphic signs of dishonesty: the letters *a, t, p, o,* and *d* are all open at the base, having been written with at least two separate strokes. Certainly no intelligent person would deliberately put such evidence into his script, so when we find it, it must be a manifestation of the subconscious.

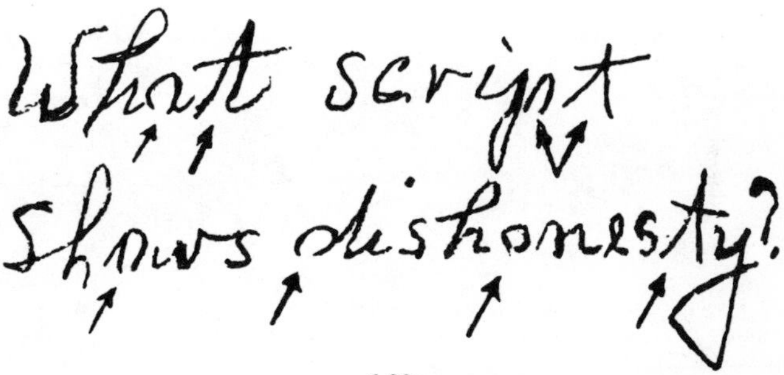

6-29

The late Dr. Robert Saudek, in his book entitled *Experiments with Handwriting* (Wm. Morrow & Co., New York, 1929, pp. 277 ff.), offers "an exact scientific method . . . by which honesty and dishonesty can be recognized from handwriting." I strongly recommend this book to anyone interested in the subject and especially to persons in personnel work.

From the above illustrations you can see why I prefer to have my clients write with something other than a cheap ball point pen. About 99 percent of the cheaper ballpoints will make a blot, a gap, a skip, or a narrow spot in the writing line that looks like a limp but is actually the result of a defect in the writing instrument and not in the writer. Occasionally, other things, such as a dent in the surface under the paper, will cause a defect.

Blots and thin spots caused by a poor ball point pen occur in almost every letter that has an upper or lower loop, usually near the point where the movement changes from an upstroke to a downward one, or vice versa. With a little experience, however, you can recognize these easily. But if the same irregularity occurs only ten or twelve times on a page, and always in a location that corresponds to the same part of the body, there is a strong likelihood that you are observing a limp and you should interpret it according to the principles given in this chapter.

Don't "play doctor" and frighten your client to death. Tell him you are not a physician and you are not infallible but urge him to have a medical examination as soon as possible, including tests for whatever his handwriting indicates is a difficulty. If you are wrong in your interpretation, he will be happy to learn that he is in good health; but if you are right, then the sooner a physician makes a correct diagnosis, the quicker the trouble can be treated or cured.

Chapter 7. What Does The Love-Arc Tell?

There is a fairly general agreement among professional graphologists as to the meaning of the slants in the downstrokes of the various letters. For instance, in *Applied Graphology* (Gregg, 1920) A. J. Smith says: "There are three forms of slope: the *right slope,* that has to do almost entirely with the affections; the *vertical,* that marks an indifference to affection; the *backhand,* which in a certain sense is a modification of the vertical hand and always indicates coldheartedness."

Ulrich Sonnemann, Ph.D., one of the most respected authors of scientific textbooks, says in *Handwriting Analysis as a Psychodiagnostic Tool* (Grune & Stratton, 1950, pp. 23, 72):

> Any movement of the arm-hand system swinging away from the body in a natural and unstrained manner necessitates the following of a rightward direction which graphologically is therefore identified as the direction of contact and of externalization per se, while emphasis on leftward movement is interpreted as significant of contact avoidance and of concentration, in whatever manner and aim, upon the self. . . . Finally, the rightward slant as an indicator of the personal need for *communication* clearly relates to all those human tendencies which *incline* toward experiences within the general area of emotional participation, of group integration, and of spiritual communion.

You can see that these two quotations agree in basic principle, even though Mr. Smith is an advocate of the out-dated "letter signs" systems of graphology, and Dr. Sonnemann was an associate professor of psychology and lecturer in the graduate faculty of City College of New York.

Every book on handwriting analysis devoted at least one chapter to

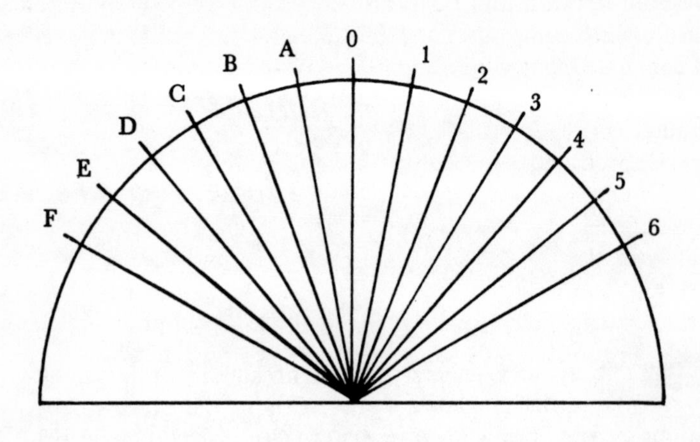

7-1

the inclination of the letters, usually displaying a diagram somewhat similar to this one above.

But nowhere have I seen any discussion that would indicate that slant Number 4, for example, had any relationship to any slant that carries a letter, in the above method of designating slopes. However, when I first started using a small two-bit plastic protractor, which did look like this diagram (although it had figures that were geometrically correct in degrees), I discovered a fact of great importance and I want to tell you how I stumbled upon it.

A great many people whose handwriting I analyzed, perhaps as many as one out of ten, said to me: "I have two different kinds of handwriting." Naturally I told these people to give me a sample of each style. Occasionally the result would be one cursive script and one printed or manuscript type. But dozens and dozens of times, the two different kinds of handwriting would be identical in every particular, except that one slanted forward and the other backward. When I actually measured with my protractor the angles of inclination in both scripts, I found that many times the person who wrote at 130° forward had a backhand slant that measured a mathematical 70°; in other words, the same person wrote at slants 4 and *B* as shown in Figure 7-1. Similarly, if the forward slant were number 5, the backhand frequently was *C;* and the correlations of 3 with *A* and of 6 with *D,* and so on, seemed to occur just as often when my client wrote both forward and backhand specimens. Occasionally a single sample would have both leftward and rightward slopes, but again I would find the measurements came out *A* and 3, or *B* and 4, or *C* and 5, respectively.

I concluded that slant *A* represented one emotional phase and slant 3 a different emotional phase of the same personality, and so on for the other correlations stated above. I suddenly realized that I needed a special protractor on which slant *A* and slant 3 would carry the same designation. Since I was using on the right half of my protractor the obtuse angles, by which slant 3 read (geometrically) 120°, then I would call slant *A* 120° and make *B, C, D,* and *E* read 130°, 140°, 150°, and 160°, respectively, to equal the slants they correlated with on the forward inclination. Seeking one-word descriptions of the three kinds of people this device measured, according to their emotional types as indicated by their writing, I decided on the three words you see on my LOVE-ARC: "CHOOSY," "COLD," and "ARDENT."

Once I decided I needed a special protractor, the obvious answer was to make one. The basic design was relatively simple, but it took me hours and hours of work to achieve it.

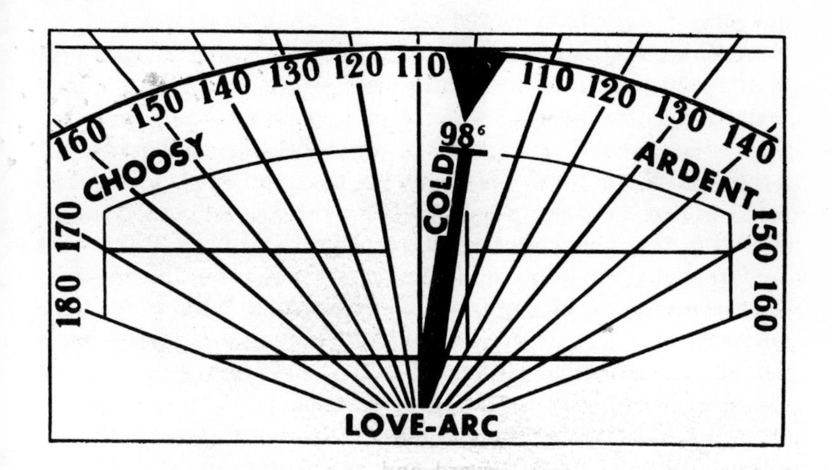

7-2

Now if you will look at the picture of my LOVE-ARC in Figure 7-2, you will see that the numbers on its right half, marked ARDENT, read 110°, 120°, 130°, 140°, 150°, and 160°, and correspond precisely to these same obtuse angles on an ordinary protractor. I never once found any writing that measured 170° or 180° in this series, so when I designed my own protractor I simply omitted these.

The use of horizontal lines is based on a theorem that every schoolboy learns during his first month in a geometry class: "If two or more parallel lines are crossed by a straight line, its angle of intersection with each parallel line are all equal." If you happen not to remember your geometry, you can easily check this by laying a ruler at a diagonal across a page which has on it ruled lines for writing. You will find that the slant of the ruler across any one of those lines is the same slant it has in crossing each of the others. This holds true no matter how many different ways you may slant the ruler.

You can slide a specimen of your handwriting under this picture of my protractor in such a way that one of these horizontal lines covers precisely the imaginary base line on which you wrote the word *details.* Let us suppose you find that the *t* in this word has the same slant as the line I have marked 130° ARDENT; you can repeat this maneuver with any other horizontal line for a base line, or you can turn the writing upside down, and the *t* will still come out with exactly the same measurement.

To correspond to the well-known figures for the I.Q. (intelligence quotient), I started calling the figures on my protractor a measurement of the "E.Q.," meaning "emotion quotient." After I began using it, and explaining that the greater the slant, the greater the relative frequency with which the writer expressed his emotions, including those of love and affection, some of my clients began jokingly to call it the "LOVE-ARC." So I promptly put those two words on the form that I sent to be copyrighted.

I want to emphasize that all the principles given you in this book are formulated in view of up-to-date interpretations of the principles of behaviorism psychology and of aptitude testing. Wherever you find interpretations here that correspond with the older system of handwriting analysis, based on "signs" (see A. J. Smith's *Applied Graphology*), such similarity is purely coincidental.

For example, we both agree that the *t*-bar that dashes off to the right of the letter means "impatience," whether or not it may touch the upright stem; it shows that the writer was too *impatient* to bring his hand from the end of the word all the way back to the proper point for starting the crossbar. But Smith gives forty (!) different forms of the letter *t,* and another writer from the same school gives twenty-eight *t*'s. I do not believe that it is possible that an exceptionally long *t*-cross could be the sign of: "Quick decisions; not thorough; apt to rush to get things done quickly." Or "Impulsiveness; an unobservant nature." Yet these are actual quotations from the books mentioned.

John B. Watson, professor of psychology at Johns Hopkins, attacked this "signs" method in his book *Psychology from the Standpoint of a Behaviorist* (Lippincott, 1919, pp. 410-411) by giving details of an experiment, a condensed version of which follows:

> The graphologists assert that they read character by such graphological signs as follows: ambition–lines of writing slope upward; perseverance–long bars on the *t*'s; reserve–closed *a*'s and *o*'s . . .
>
> The subjects were seventeen students of the University of Wisconsin belonging to the same medical fraternity. Each man was first asked to write in his ordinary manner a paragraph from a popular magazine. . . . When the writing was finished the subject was given a set of sixteen small cards each containing the name of one of the other subjects, his own name not being included. He was directed to arrange the cards in the order of the amount of *ambition* possessed by the persons indicated on each. A ranking was thus obtained. The writing was then subjected to measurement, the *m*'s, *n*'s, and *t*'s were especially measured and the ranking for ambition correlated with the pronounced upward slope of the lines of writing or the reverse. A statistical measure showed no tendency whatever for the ambitious person to write in an upward sloping direction. . . . No correlation could be found with respect to *perseverance* and the length of the bars on the *t*'s. There was no correlation between closing of the *a*'s and *o*'s and *reserve.*
>
> The tests upon these students thus gave only negative results. When one examines the whole mass of literature bearing upon personality studies of these kinds, one is soon convinced that it is a tissue of exaggeration and that the so-called results will not bear critical experimental testing.

Such experiments as the one quoted above and the studies of such authors as Ludwig Klages, Hans J. Jacoby, Max Pulver, Robert Saudek, Ulrich Sonnemann, and Werner Wolff, among many others, prove that the older system of graphology, based on "signs," is unscientific and inaccurate.

I think the most concise summary of this older system is contained in Smith's *Applied Graphology,* mentioned earlier. Published in 1920, it is now out of print, and I consider that it was ten years out of date when it appeared, because in 1910 Klages published *The Problems of Graphology* (in Leipzig), a study based on the observation of expressive movements or "gestures" in handwriting. This was the first treatise on the subject that was in accord with the behaviorism principles that form part of modern psychology. This older, outdated system of analyzing handwriting is still being used by thousands of amateur graphologists throughout the United States and by a few professionals.

I will confess that when I first became seriously interested in doing handwriting analysis I took the trouble to memorize some eighty pages of Smith's book. Quite by accident, I had found that people I met at parties were much amused by the two or three things I could tell them about themselves by looking at their handwriting. A whole new path to social popularity suddenly opened before me. I bought a secondhand copy of Smith and spent an average of two hours of study every day for a solid year. I bought a pack of three-by-five-inch index cards; across the top of each I put in my own handwriting an example from his book. Beneath that I typed his description of the "sign," such as "impatient *t*," "lying *t*," "talkative *t*," "sense-of-humor *t*," and so on. Then underneath I typed exactly what he said each of these meant.

As I used my newly acquired talent more and more at parties, I began to work out a formula which I have since applied quite successfully as a professional entertainer. I would tell each person only the eight to ten traits I thought were most clearly indicated by his writing. But even when I followed Smith accurately, I soon found I was lucky if as many as half of these were accepted by the writer as being correct.

To cover my mistakes I started to use, for each trait I mentioned, any clever phrase or gag that seemed to be reasonably appropriate. So I went over my three-by-five-inch index cards and carefully typed on each one a sentence or two that contained a distinctive or humorous way of emphasizing the given characteristic; for instance, for stubbornness: "You set your foot down as deep as a telephone pole." This one gets a chuckle about nine times out of ten, so I have been using it for more than a dozen years. Whenever I use one several times without any laughs, I discard it and try another one. As W. C. Fields once said: "Who knows what's funny?"

The LOVE-ARC proved a great help to me in my efforts to be entertaining; no one had ever seen such a thing before, and I was able to explain it in a convincing manner. I had my printer make me some pads with my picture in cartoon-style on each page, as shown in Figure 7-3. Underneath my picture there was a facsimile of my own signature and some wording: "Hal Falcon, Ph.D., says the degree of your love-fever is:" and immediately after the colon I would write the *maximum* slant shown in their handwriting specimens, as measured by my special protractor, such as "130° CHOOSY" or "150° ARDENT." Some clients set such store by these that they carried them around for years; they would bring a friend in to see me months and sometimes years after I had done their analysis, and say: "Look, Johnny, the professor told me my love-fever was 140° but I'm awfully choosy about using it. Let's see what he says about your writing."

says the degree of your love-fever is:

7-3

When you apply the LOVE-ARC to your own specimen, using the illustration in Figure 7-2, you must remember *two* things: (1) the slant of the writing represents the *frequency* with which you express your emotions, and (2) the amount of the pressure in your writing indicates the *intensity* with which you express these emotions.

Now if the majority of letters in your own sample slant at, say, 130°–140° ARDENT, then when you wrote you were leaning these letters away from yourself and toward other people. Such a heavy slant forward represents basically outgoing emotions, expressed often and with enthusiasm (that is, ARDENT-ly). It indicates that you lean *toward people,* emotionally; in general, you prefer people face-to-face rather than as an audience for which you perform. So persons of your type are gregarious and they do well in occupations where they deal with individuals among the general public. They not only do a good job in sales or personnel departments, they do well as receptionists, airline stewardesses, waiters, bellmen, and other hotel employees, and as clerks in stores. With enough "power" and intelligence, such persons can succeed as executives or owners of businesses where they employ workers in the above categories.

On the other hand, if you find a script which measures, say, 130° CHOOSY, then in the act of writing that person was inclining his letters away from people and back toward himself. This means that many times he gets "fed up" with people and then, like Greta Garbo, he "vants to be alawn"—and he can be alone without being lonely. This is a quality he shares with all creative people and with most geniuses. If a man wants to paint a picture, write a poem or a short story, or perfect an invention, he does not seek a noisy, crowded room. Instead, he gets off by himself, in an office, a studio, a den, or a laboratory; any person who works with him must be only an additional pair of hands for his help and never a disturbing influence. Such a man is CHOOSY in at least three different ways:

1. He chooses carefully, as an artist or inventor, his designs, his colors, his wording, his materials, his planned results.

2. He chooses with great care anything he considers *important* to himself and for himself; this may include his clothes, his car, his home, his tools, his golf clubs, or any or none of these, but he *always* selects with utmost care his friends (not acquaintances, but his "real buddies," if he has any at all).

3. He chooses always, when with other people, to express the emotional attitude he considers suitable for the occasion rather than the one he actually feels; that is, when not alone he is always "putting on an act," even if he refuses to admit this to himself.

Now since my special protractor is labeled LOVE-ARC, I want to tell you how it can help you in the realm of romance. Instead of the terms CHOOSY and ARDENT, which I use, you may substitute such terms as introvert and extrovert, nongregarious and gregarious, defiant and compliant, self-oriented and other-oriented, or perhaps self-centered and considerate. I do not regard CHOOSY and ARDENT as expressing direct opposites, but each constitutes the best one-word description I could find of the outstanding characteristic of people who write, respectively, backhand or forward slants. If you can think of other words you consider more suitable than mine, by all means use them.

Remember that psychologists say no person is 100 percent introvert or extrovert, except in infancy or an insane asylum. A newly-born infant is a good example of a 100 percent introvert; he acts as if he is so self-centered that he thinks the entire world and all the people in it exist solely for the purpose of supplying his wants. He cries when he wants something, having absolutely no consideration for anyone but himself. From the instant he becomes aware that he and his mother are separate persons and that there are other people in the world, his whole life must be devoted to learning by experience, often painful experience, how to "adjust" so as to live among people and to get along with them. His very existence depends on his learning this quite unwelcome lesson, and his success in any occupation often depends on precisely the extent to which he proves he has learned it.

Every person old enough to talk is, therefore, a complicated mixture of introvert and extrovert, however you may define these terms. There is even a somewhat newer term, "ambivert," created to apply to those people who show that they are approximately half introvert and half extrovert.

The type of person who writes two different styles, one CHOOSY and one ARDENT, is indicating characteristics that might cause some analysts to label him "ambivert." In general, I would classify the person who consistently writes backhanded as self-seeking, or self-centered, rather than selfish—or, if you prefer the terms, as egoistic rather than egotistic. To illustrate my point, let me give you an example of what I mean, put into greatly oversimplified terms.

Let's assume that a self-centered person buys a pie. He will divide it into five pieces. No matter how much he loves his wife, he will always give her two pieces and keep three for himself. If he habitually gave her three and kept only two, that would indicate that he was *not* self-centered. In other words, to him "being fair" means always 60 percent for him and 40 percent for the other.

If two self-centered people marry each other, even if for some reason they do make a fifty-fifty split on everything, each one invariably ends up feeling cheated because he is not getting what he considers his rightful due. Each is somewhat like the youngster who told his slightly older brother, who demanded half of his apple: "You're just a selfish old meanie because you don't want me to have it all!"

This is one reason why so many marriages between successful performers in the entertainment world break up so quickly. The same self-seeking drive that made them stars in the first place has made them totally unsuitable as a romantic partner for another person of the same general type. Let me tell you a true story to illustrate this, although the persons involved were in no way connected with any form of show business.

In New York, over a dozen years ago, a client who had often brought in friends to have their writing analyzed brought me a page of a letter and, at my request, he let me look at the signature at the bottom of the last page also. He said: "I'm getting married next month, so tell me what you think of her."

I looked at the script: it was 130° CHOOSY, #1 pressure, very slow writing, with relatively little libido. I was familiar with my client's own writing: 140° CHOOSY, #7 pressure, medium speed, with many indications of a strong sex urge. He made his living selling coal to industrial plants. Now you will need only to compare the pressure and slant in the one script with that in the other and you will know just what my answer was: "If you want the real truth, Don, the kindest thing I can tell you is: don't marry her under any circumstances. She has precisely the wrong kind of personality to fit in with your own. You two are much too much alike in many respects to get along well together. The right type of girl for you is one whose writing is as unlike yours as possible; it should certainly have slants as far to the right as your script goes to the left."

Well, my client married her anyhow, the very next month, and for five solid years he refused to speak to me even if we passed close enough to touch. Then one evening, after I had not seen him for a couple of years, he came in to see me to have his handwriting analyzed again. Afterward we chatted awhile, as we had done on previous occasions, and almost apologetically he told me his story.

He and his wife were miserably unhappy. They fought endlessly over insignificant matters, such as how many inches a window should be left open at night. Just recently they had moved into separate bedrooms.

"If it wasn't for the two children and our religion I'd get a divorce," he said. "Although I couldn't get it in this state. The only grounds I could give is complete incompatibility."

In my opinion, the clash of personalities that made his story an unhappy one was due to the fact that they were both the type that I call CHOOSY. On the other hand, if two people are both the type I call ARDENT, and are very much in love when they marry, each will try to give the other three slices of pie and keep only two—or, if you prefer arithmetical terms, each will try to give 60 percent and take only 40 percent. By some nonmathematical magic, this will add up to at least 120 percent of happiness for the two of them; other things being equal, such marriages may well last a lifetime.

The characters in O. Henry's *The Gift of the Magi* exemplify the ARDENT types; you will recall that the story concerns a bride who cuts off and sells her long hair to buy a watch chain as a Christmas gift to adorn the prized heirloom watch that her husband has sold without her knowledge, in order to buy a comb for her lovely hair.

It follows, obviously, that a CHOOSY person should never marry any except an ARDENT one, and even then the marriage is likely to be successful and happy only if the latter is willing always to give the 60 percent freely and accept the 40 percent for his own share, without in any way feeling hurt, cheated, resentful, or sorry for himself. As the French so aptly say: "There is always one who kisses, and one who holds the cheek."

So if you want a happy marriage, and if your writing is in the ARDENT category, check scripts with my LOVE-ARC until you find one that reads 120°–150° ARDENT, with at least 10°–20° more slant than yours. Remember that the pressure of the man's writing should measure at least two grades more than the woman's, because if his is only equal to hers, or is lighter, then on some occasions he will react to a situation in a way that she is bound to consider weak or namby-pamby. The heavier her writing is, the less likely is she to tolerate a husband that she thinks of as weak. Subject to this limitation and to the further precaution that a person whose writing is beyond 155° ARDENT may be too extreme for his own good, or yours, follow this guide: If you would rather be more loved than loving, then pick yourself a mate whose writing is 120° ARDENT or more, preferably one with at least ten degrees more slant than yours. For sexual considerations, see chapter 10.

Chapter 8. *What's Your Slant On Life?*

In studying the inclination of the letters in the specimen of your handwriting, you must interpret correctly two different things: (1) the *average* of all the slants of the measurable letters and (2) the *maximum* slant shown by any one letter.

The slant of a single letter could be the result of an accident caused by a movement of the paper or of the writing table, so for the maximum slant I would take the heaviest angle that I could find repeated, say, at least three times in measurable letters. Especially I would apply this precaution if I had available a whole page of writing as a specimen, instead of a single sentence.

The average of all the slants gives you the writer's habitual pattern of emotional expression, and therefore gives you a guide to the type of occupation at which he is most likely to be successful. The maximum slant, as determined above, shows his extreme frequency of expression as impelled by a very strong emotion such as anger, joy, fear, sorrow, anxiety, or love and affection. In most cases the difference between

Write: Handwriting
tells 2,458 details!

8-1 VERSATILITY: slants vary from 140° CHOOSY–105° ARDENT: as singer, he won scholarship at Juilliard; after two years, studied physics and chemistry on scholarship at another school; now wants to become a professional portrait photographer.

the average and the maximum, as here described, will be no more than 5°–10°, but I have seen a few cases where they were as much as thirty points apart. This latter circumstance would indicate a person who is normally very much self-controlled, and perhaps even repressed, but who sometimes boils over into an emotional state that would astonish associates who may have known him for years without ever having seen such an "explosion."

Above I have mentioned "measurable" letters. Theoretically the slant of every letter is to be considered, but it is quite difficult and unnecessary to measure the slant of small letters such as *a, o, u, n,* and *m.* Usually I measure only the slope of long letters such as *b, d, f, g, h, j,* and so on. I would not bother with any of the smaller letters mentioned unless their slant was noticeably different from that of the looped ones, and I cannot recall ever having seen a script where this was true.

To obtain a strictly scientific average, you would have to measure every single loop letter, put down its degree of inclination, add up all the figures, and then divide by the number of letters measured. Perhaps you should do this on your own specimen and on two or three others at first, just for practice. But with experience you will learn to pick out quickly three to six representative long letters, measure the slants of these, and make a rapid mental calculation as to their average. I use the figure I obtain in this manner as an indication of the type of occupation for which the client best seems suited (this will be discussed further later in the chapter), but I usually do not mention anything to him about the difference between the average and the maximum slants in his writing.

What I do explain to every client is the difference between letters that lean toward other people and those that lean back toward the writer and what this difference means. To show him how it is done, I usually measure the three or four letters in his script that appear to have the heaviest slant, take the figure that represents the largest number of degrees among these, and write it down on the pad as his "E.Q." (emotion quotient) or "Love-fever"—I use the two terms as synonyms.

I always explain that this figure represents the maximum frequency of expression for *all* powerful emotions, not just for those of love and affection.

The basic principles underlying this study of slants—namely, a rightward slant represents a leaning toward people and therefore implies frequency of expression or willingness to express an emotion;

and the leftward slant means a great deal of choosiness as to how, when, where, and with what or with whom emotion will be expressed, if at all—apply to other gestures of the body fully as much as to handwriting.

8-2 Variation in slant from 145° CHOOSY–125° ARDENT: coming from Asia, he took B.S. (chemistry) at one school, B.S. (pre-medical) at another, M.D. at a third, then Ph.D. (biochemistry) at a fourth; now does teaching and research elsewhere.

As the late Hans J. Jacoby says in his book *Self-Knowledge Through Handwriting* (Dent & Sons, Ltd., London, 1941, p. 34): "A man who is carried away by the speaker will lean forward as if wanting to meet him; another by leaning back, seems to recoil from him in an effort to escape and ward off his influence; the upright position shows neither sympathy with the lecturer nor its opposite—it is the attitude of the self-sufficient person."

Now let us look once more at the specimen of your writing that you prepared according to previous instructions. You should have written on unlined paper, but a line that connected the lowest point of each of the small letters in a single word would be more or less straight, but not necessarily horizontal: you may have written diagonally across the page. Start at any point on this base line of the word and draw another short line upwards at a right angle, that is, perpendicular to the base. We consider any letters that are approximately parallel to this perpendicular line as vertical or upright, even though they may not be so in relation to the bottom of the page. Letters that lean to the right of this line we describe as having a rightward or forward slope; letters that lean to its left we call backhand or leftward slanting.

Some people, in an effort to achieve individuality, write their signatures on a line running uphill at about a 45-degree angle; often they will write a brief message in a similar manner. The point to remember here is that the line of reference for measuring the slant of

that government of the people;
le, for the people, shall not per=
he earth.

Abraham Lincoln.

November 19. 1863.

8-3 Coordination shown by straight lines and accurate placement of commas and periods.

letters in such a script is the base line of the word in which the letter appears and not the edge of the paper.

If the lowest points of all small letters in one of your words form a perfectly straight base line, this indicates that you have good coordination. If similar bases of all words you put in one line of writing lie in a single straight line (the line may run uphill or downhill across the page), this also demonstrates coordination. And if the colon, the four figures, the comma in the figure, and the period under the exclamation point all rest accurately on this single straight line, then you probably rank exceptionally high in coordination. Other indications of this trait are discussed in chapter 5.

Now let me repeat: the slant that you measure in any letter is always the angle it makes with the base line of the word in which it occurs. Therefore, if someone writes on a torn piece of wrapping paper or on something round like a paper picnic plate you can still measure the slant of his letters by this method.

Concerning the "uphill" and "downhill" lines of writing mentioned above, let me quote Sonnemann (*op. cit.,* pp. 92-96) at this point:

> Indications of a feeling of optimism, zeal, "elevation," suggest themselves for rising lines. . . . This suggests its particular closeness to the momentary emotional conditions experienced by the writer . . . The line "falls" whenever the arm of the person . . . gradually sinks

> back toward the body . . . and its psychological correlate, discouragement or depression, will suggest itself. . . . The steady horizontal line, accordingly, is the product of attitudes not significantly influenced by the swerving effects of uncontrolled emotion.

Sonnemann also suggests that slightly downhill lines occurring after several pages of writing "is simply the common consequence of normal muscular fatigue." Smith and others of the "old school" say that base lines that parallel the bottom edge of the paper are "general significations for . . . honesty and straightforwardness," but I agree with Sonnemann that, instead, this indicates an even temperament not easily influenced by elation or depression.

It is my experience that a person who writes consistently downhill on the sentence I ask for as a specimen is unhappy at that moment because of some condition or problem he faces, for which he sees at that time no satisfactory solution. In my earliest days as a professional analyst, I memorized a sentence that summarizes all this: "A level line means a level head; uphill for optimism, downhill for discouragement."

But whether it goes uphill or down, the base line of a particular word is still the reference from which you measure the slant of any letter in it. I find that whenever I mention the slant of writing in a group of people, someone is likely to bring up the very widespread theory that all backhand writing is done with the left hand and that all those who write with the left hand write a backhand. My experience indicates that this theory is completely false. Many right-handers write a backhand. *If* the writer is permitted to move the paper around to any position that pleases him, there is absolutely no correlation whatsoever between backhand writing and the use of the left hand, under ordinary circumstances.

There is one way you can detect that writing is done with the left hand, if you do not watch it being written: about 80 percent of all left-handed writing contains a *t*-bar made from right to left. Some-

8-4 Dancer, dance instructor, and choreographer; left-handed writing.

times you may need a magnifying glass to determine this, but the blunt end of such a bar is its beginning and the pointed end is its finish. So if the sharp point of several *t*-crosses is toward the left of the page, the writing was done with the left hand; no right-hander crosses his *t*'s in such a manner.

There is some correlation between a forward slant and the speed with which the writing is done. If you will try it, you will find that the fastest stroke you can make in handwriting is an almost straight horizontal, such as a long cross-bar on a *t*. Such a line, when used under a signature to emphasize it, is usually made at very high speed.

The next fastest stroke is a somewhat wavy line, such as banks urge that you use to fill in a blank space on a check you have written. For instance, if you try to take down verbatim a lecture or a telephone conversation by writing much faster in longhand than you normally do, you will find that syllables commonly ending words, such as *-ion, -son* and *-ing,* tend to become just such horizontal wavy lines or wiggles. Especially signatures written at high speed tend to degenerate into mere wiggly lines. Harassed executives, who must sign hundreds of bulletins, memos, or letters in a rush each afternoon, often develop just such a signature; it is usually quite illegible.

Also, when you try to write much faster than usual, your long letters will incline somewhat more toward the forward horizontal. On the other hand, the slowest writing tends to lean well to the left, around 150° CHOOSY on the LOVE-ARC. Vertical script tends to be written much slower than script that leans forward. And if you try to disguise your writing in any way, you are likely to produce a specimen written at much less than your normal speed. The most common attempt at disguising handwriting is merely a change of slant, say, a backhand instead of the usual forward inclination—but all the letter shapes and other habitual characteristics remain unchanged.

So far in this discussion I have spoken of the vertical, that is, a perpendicular to the base line of the word, as being the dividing point between backhand and forward slant. This is the normal usage of these words, not only among the public in general, but by almost all writers on graphology, although one graphologist says he "considers the vertical as a form of backhand." Mathematically, of course, the perpendicular is the correct point of division between inclinations to the left or right, and it might be psychologically true in a country where the prevailing slant of writing taught in the schools was vertical. But with two minor exceptions, all of the systems of writing taught in schools in the United States (Spencerian, Mills, Palmer, Zaner-

Blosser, to name a few) use a distinct forward slant, which is considered the easiest and most natural style for right-handed people, as the great majority of pupils are. I have measured the slants in the copybooks of these systems, and without exception they are 120°–140° ARDENT as measured by my LOVE-ARC (corresponding to acute angles with the base line of 60°–40°). I have not personally checked all the systems of writing taught in European countries, but I believe almost all of them also prescribe a forward slant at a similar angle.

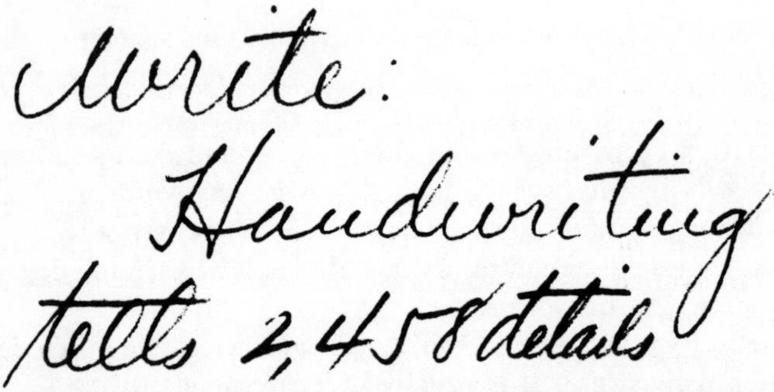

8-5 120° ARDENT: attorney specializing in tax and finance; won medal for Palmer method penmanship in high school and one for marksmanship in the Army.

In my opinion, this habitual writing of rightward slopes in childhood deflects the psychological dividing point between backhand and forward slants by a distance, which I have estimated from my own experience, of approximately 9° to the right of vertical, that is, at an obtuse angle of about 99° clockwise from the base line of the word. This figure comes so close to equalling the 98.6° familiar to most Americans as the Fahrenheit temperature marked on fever thermometers as normal for the body, that I put this better known figure on my LOVE-ARC. To avoid getting into long technical discussions with clients who question me about it, I fend them off with a quip: "If your temperature falls much below that, you're dead and I'm only interested in *live* ones—corpses can't write."

So by empirical data drawn from my own personal experience in making many thousands of analyses, the psychological "dead center" that indicates the least amount of emotional *expression* is represented on my LOVE-ARC (pictured in Figure 7-2 in the preceding chapter) as a point marked 98.6° of circular measurement. I drew in a heavy line there and marked it "COLD," meaning "lacking in the expression of emotion."

8-6 Librarian's script.

To go back to the two minor exceptions among writing systems mentioned above, the most common one by far is the stilted vertical or slight backhand—120° CHOOSY—that all librarians apparently must learn. It is extremely legible, but rather slow in execution; it sometimes has the letters disconnected, as in printing or manuscript styles. You will normally find many examples of it among the index cards filed in any public library (see Figure 8-6).

The other exception is a distinct leftward slope, often as much as 140° CHOOSY, frequently taught in parochial schools for girls, especially those conducted by communities of the Sacred Heart or of Our Lady of the Lake. When I worked in Houston, San Antonio, Dallas, San Diego, and other cities in the Southwest, it was often possible to identify instantly a graduate of one of these schools by her style of writing. As far as I have been able to learn, the emotional attitudes that the good sisters tried to drill into their young charges are precisely those that are indicated by this style of writing. Perhaps it is a great compliment to the efficiency with which they do this drilling that some twenty years after her graduation from such a convent school a woman will recognize it as an accurate description of herself when, if she is still using this basic style, I tell her the traits that this type of writing indicates.

This brings up another point: if you analyze the writing of someone who is less than, say, five years away from his last class in penmanship, you cannot always be sure just which traits shown apply to the individual and which are merely an imitation of his school copybook. Of course, the variations from the original style learned are what indicate his particular traits, and the more individualistic and unconventional he is, the more quickly he will develop these variations. For example, if a schoolteacher writes such a perfect specimen of Palmer script that it can be photographed for use in a textbook for teaching such penmanship, it tells us very little excecpt that she is extraordinarily well coordinated to be able to reproduce it so accurately.

But consider this well-known fact: if five girls are classmates who graduate the same day from the same shorthand class taught by the same teacher, then approximately five years later no one of them can transcribe from any of the notes written by any one of the others. Similarly, if they all learn penmanship at the same time in the same class from the same teacher, then five years or more later their scripts will show enough individual variations to give you a great deal of information about their personalities.

In general it is possible to correlate certain slants with an aptitude for certain occupations. Here again this is based on empirical data, that is, on my personal observations made in analyzing the writing of thousands of men and women who actually make a living by working in the fields cited. You will find many individual exceptions, of course; some of them because occasionally a person will get into a field for which he is not really suited. But with a little experience in using the information in the rest of this chapter, you can be accurate about 80 percent of the time in describing the general type of occupation for which an individual is best adapted. You will be able to amaze your subjects by the frequency with which the facts verify that he is actually working in some phase of that field. The more successful the people you analyze, of course, the more likely it is that this will be true.

Now here are the categories, given in terms of the average of the slants marked on the LOVE-ARC, and my comments on each.

1) 98.6° COLD. If all the measurable letters averaged out at this slant on my protractor, and especially if no one of them inclined much beyond the 110° mark on either side of it, such writing indicates an extremely stoical person who tends to repress rigidly any expression of emotion whatsoever. If this were a woman's script, and

Dear Hal,
What does my
handwriting tell you?

8-7 98.6° COLD: professional musician, still virgin at thirty-three, despite the fact that she is a redhead.

especially if the pressure were only #2 or less, I would consider her a "born old maid," if this term could ever be applied properly to any woman.

A man with such writing, but with pressure of #3 or #4, might well be the kind of money-lender who is reputed to have ice water in his veins instead of blood. I have never met, knowingly, a professional hangman or executioner of either the legal or the gangster type, but this is the kind of writing I would expect from a person in such an occupation, though with a pressure of at least #5 or #6 or heavier. Writing of this type with pressure ranging up to #10 is what I would expect of the professional gambler who could bet his entire fortune on the turn of a card, lose it, and nonchantly light a cigarette without the slightest visible expression of emotion.

Please note the emphasis on *expression* of emotion. Letters made at this angle with considerable pressure, #5 or heavier, indicate *not* absence of emotion, but *control* of emotion. A person who writes like this may, in the course of a discussion or negotiation or poker game, experience a whole range of emotions, from joy to excitement to fear to anger and back again, and yet never reveal a single one of these emotions by any word, gesture, or facial expression.

2) 110° ARDENT. This kind of writing indicates the auditor, the investigator, the scientist. It could be the type of auditor who would send his own brother to jail for embezzlement if he uncovered the evidence of it, or perhaps an investigator who would pin a murder on

Write: Handwriting tells
2,458 details! Gold

8-8 110° ARDENT: physicist.

Write: Handwriting
tells 2,458 Details!

8-9 120° ARDENT: activist C.P.A., who became treasurer and now also president of textile-making factory.

a close friend or relative, by persistently seeking evidence that would lead to conviction. In the world of science this style might be that of a chemist trained in criminology whose work often results in sending men to the electric chair by the accuracy with which he determines traces of poison or analyzes blood stains.

3) 120° ARDENT. Among men whose script shows an average (this is not the maximum, remember) slant at this angle, I frequently find those who deal professionally with money: bank loan officers, mortgage-lenders, comptrollers, and treasurers of corporations (many of them C.P.A.'s), credit managers, floor traders on the stock exchange, bond-issue buyers for brokerage houses, and those who buy raw materials, tools, and equipment, especially when these must meet exacting specifications.

Since I have mentioned "buyers," I want to explain that this term is applied in big department stores to the person who is actually a sales manager for a certain department, even though he (or, more frequently, *she*) does buy the merchandise for that division. Such an individual is much more likely to write with an average slope of 140° ARDENT, with very heavy pressure.

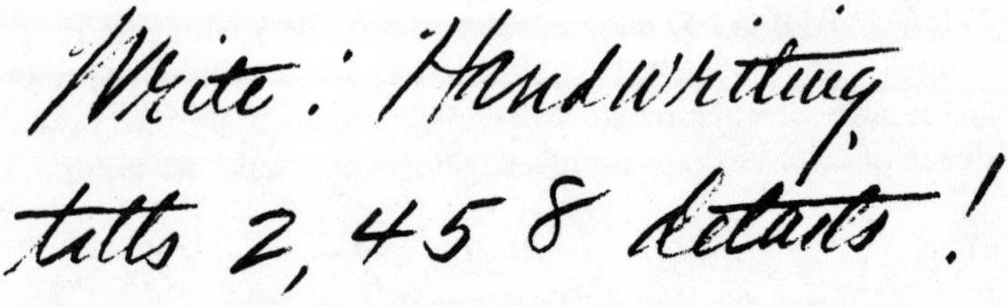

8-10 130° ARDENT: attorney, Phi Beta Kappa; went from general counsel to president of shipping company.

4) 130° ARDENT. This classification includes all the managerial group, ranging from foreman all the way up to personnel director, vice-president, general manager, or captain of industry. Men of this type usually make better general managers than they do sales managers, although some of them may have a background in selling or sales management. Here too we find professional men who are the heads of divisions in big corporations: the chief engineer or "vice-president for engineering," the chief legal counselor, the medical director of a hospital or of a life insurance company, or the dean of a medical school faculty. The executive skills such positions require are relatively rare among men practicing a profession, but those who have

them frequently indicate this fact in their writing by exceptional pressure (#6 to #10), with an average inclination approximating 130° ARDENT.

There are no hard and fast dividing lines between these groups, of course, and you will get many borderline cases. For instance, you might find a younger executive who currently is head of the credit or the buying department of his company, with slants in his writing that average 125° ARDENT, just halfway between the "money man" and the managers. If there is enough intelligence and "power" in his script, I would say that this man is more likely in the future to develop into a general manager than to stay among his present colleagues in the financial area.

Many people change the slant of their writing over the years, and my experience indicates that the change tends to increase the number that represents the average slope as measured on the LOVE-ARC. In other words, five or ten years from now the average angle in the writing of those men who now show 125° ARDENT is much more likely to be 130° or 135° than 120° or 115° in that same direction. This may mean, in psychological terms, that a man becomes more skillful in dealing with people, more adept in communication, more

8-11 130° CHOOSY in high school to 130° ARDENT as an office manager; she started work as a secretary.

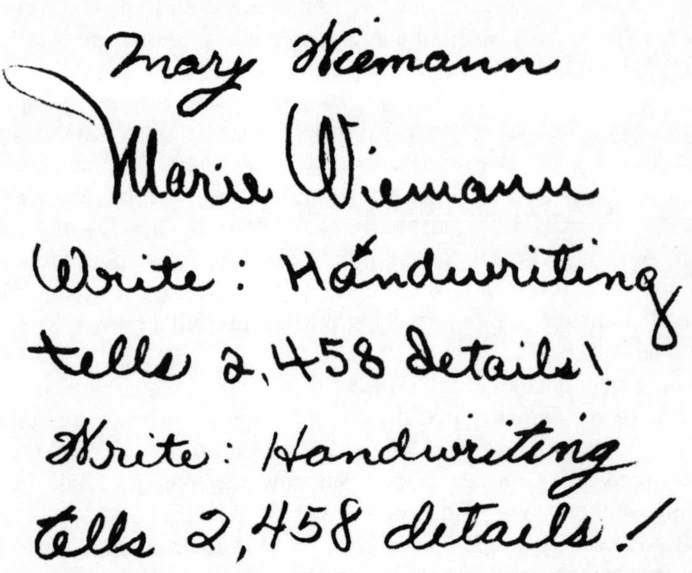

8-12 110° ARDENT as a cashier, she changed to 110° CHOOSY as a model, after winning a beauty contest.

expressive of emotion, more considerate of others, and more extrovert, as he gains maturity through experience, and this change shows in his writing.

Among the clients I have mentioned who have two distinct styles that differ only in that one slants forward and the other is backhand, I find that the backhand slant is generally the older of the two; that is, the leftward slope is the one they used when they were about high school or college age and the rightward slant started being used in their early twenties and is being used more and more as they grow older.

I can recall only two exceptions: one was a girl barely old enough to vote, working as a cashier in a store; when she won a beauty contest and embarked upon a career as a model and TV bit-player, she promptly adopted a distinct backhand script. Figure 8-12 shows both of her styles of writing.

The other exception was a similar case. When I first analyzed this girl's writing a dozen years ago, she was working five days a week as a stenographer and had a quite ordinary script that matched that occupation perfectly. But she also showed me at that time a quite different script that slanted at about 110° CHOOSY, indicating much

but am freezing! Haven't been
warm since I got off the plane
in London! Oh well, at least it's healthy.

very good. Will be in touch with
you as soon as we get back.
Hope Hal is doing well.
Love to you both—

8-13 125° ARDENT as a secretary to 110° CHOOSY as an actress; unmarried.

dramatic talent, considerable originality, and a yen for the spotlight. I told her all this. She said she had wanted to be an actress all through her teens, but she abandoned her ambition because of her family's opposition. I pointed out that she was then fully an adult, being her own boss in her own apartment and supporting herself; I suggested she take up Little Theater work as a hobby. A few years later she went even further: she studied at the Theater Wing, graduated, played summer stock several seasons, and is now a character actress who does stenography a couple of days a week to help make rent money when she is between acting jobs. The style of writing she uses most these days is, naturally, the backhand. (Figure 8-13)

The Quaker Oats Co
Merchandise Mart
Chicago Ill

8-14 140° ARDENT: sales manager for a large corporation.

5) 140° ARDENT. This average slant is characteristic of the sales managers, the merchandise managers, and buyers in big department stores, insurance general agents, jobbers, food brokers, and the owners or general managers of sales-type businesses, either wholesale or retail: jobbing houses, stores, hotels, motels, filling stations, restaurants, travel agencies, and other establishments that sell to the public in general.

In this group we also find those employees of any business which must deal with the public face-to-face. The younger people in this group, those with plenty of "power" and intelligence, will be top echelon executives of such businesses some ten to twenty years from now. I also find that lawyers with ♯6 or heavier pressure, whose

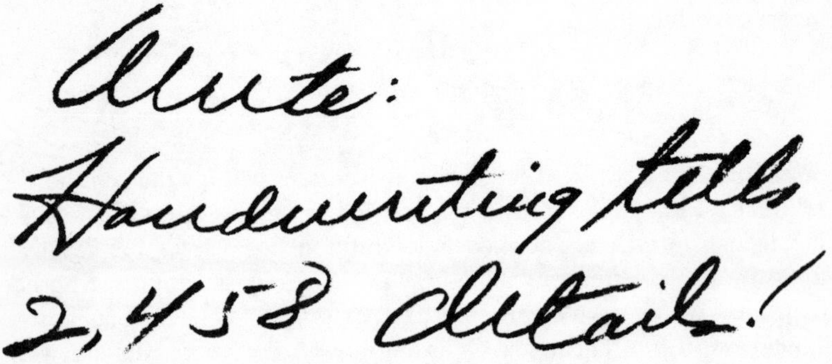

8-15 140° ARDENT: lady buyer for ladies' wear store.

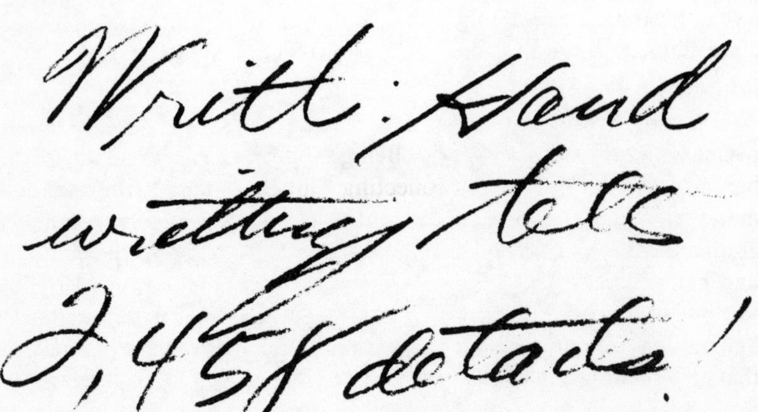

8-16 150° ARDENT: star salesman *not* recommended for sales management.

writing puts them in this category or the next, often do quite well in politics, either as candidates themselves or as "king-makers" who control political organizations.

6) 150° ARDENT. In this category, if the pressure is heavy enough, we find the star salesman, like the life insurance personal producer who does not want to become a general agent and should not be one. One reason that people who write like this frequently do well in selling is that they are so expressive of the emotions they feel; their facial expressions, their gestures, even the tones of their voices unconsciously advertise over and over again how enthusiastic they are about the products they are offering. So if your writing shows slants that average close to 140° or 150° ARDENT, stay away from poker games or any other activities that might be handicapped by an expressive face!

8-17 160° ARDENT: oversexed woman.

7) 160° ARDENT. I can recall only two people, among clients I have met in twenty years of studying and practicing graphology, whose writing averaged this degree of slant; both admitted that they had, on two or three separate occasions, been patients in a mental institution.

One was a prostitute. She told me she had been "tremendously oversexed" even before puberty. Being tall for her age, she had started her professional career by collecting "lunch money" from schoolmates and high schoolers when only twelve years old, and quickly graduated to older boys who had more money to offer. She said she had had several offers of marriage but declined them all because, as she put it, "I could never find a man who could keep me satisfied." She made it a point to know lots of football players, she explained, so that any evening she didn't feel like working, or that her soliciting had been unsuccessful, she could phone a couple of them to come over and see her; she implied it took at least two to solace her loneliness!

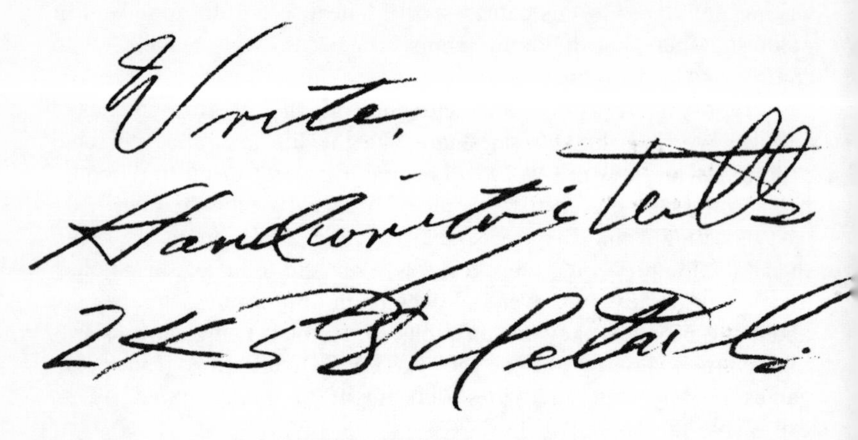

8-18 160° ARDENT: kleptomaniac.

The man who wrote with such heavy slants and very heavy pressure said he was a kleptomaniac, a shoplifter, whose parents kept him out of jail by paying for all his thefts. He, too, had never been married and had never held a regular job of any kind.

By now you have probably noticed that all of the occupations cited under these ARDENT categories have one thing in common: they all require dealing with *people* face-to-face. On the other hand, the CHOOSY categories cited below include persons who express their emotions by dealing with *things;* if they must deal with people, they prefer to meet them as an audience or to contact them indirectly, such as through the printed page. For example, a poet in love, who writes with a beautifully rhythmic backhand script, may spend hours composing a sonnet "to his lady's lovely lips"; his activist rival, however, who writes with a similarly slanted forward style, will spend the same number of hours actually kissing those same lovely lips.

Write: Handwriting
tells 2,458 details!

8-19 110° CHOOSY: vertical script of a professional writer of scientific articles for a firm of management consultants.

8) 110° CHOOSY. As you can readily see on the LOVE-ARC, this is not really a slant but is a perpendicular, forming a geometric angle of 90° with the base line. Yet my experience indicates that people whose letters average at this slant belong with those who write backhand. In general, the occupations of persons whose emotion quotient is correctly measured by the left half of my protractor tend to represent the research, philosophical, creative, or dramatic aspect of those activities that carry the corresponding numbers on the right half of the protractor.

The person whose script averages 110° CHOOSY may be a research scientist or a specialist in mathematics or statistics. If there is enough pressure to suggest leadership, he might make an efficient director of research in a big laboratory. He could easily be a teacher or an author of textbooks on auditing or on making cool appraisals of real estate.

8-20 120° CHOOSY: dancer turned interior decorator, she has two patents, one on special slipper for toe dancers.

9) 120° CHOOSY. This category correlates with 120° ARDENT, which indicates a person who handles money or the papers that represent money, such as a bank official. In Detroit, years ago, I analyzed the writing of a man who wrote a fairly consistent slope of 120° CHOOSY, including his connected, executive signature, with #7 pressure and a few breaks indicating inventiveness. By now you must know what these details mean and what I told him about them. As I usually do when I can spare the time, I chatted with him a few minutes afterward.

"I *am* the head man in a financial business," he said with enthusiasm. "I'm senior vice-president of the —— National Bank down the street. I don't know why the pressure in my writing would mean I was an athlete, but I did make three letters at college and I'm still proud of my golf handicap. Whatever gave you the idea that I was persistent enough to go to night school for something I wanted I can't imagine, but I did. Right after graduation I started to work for the bank, and I decided I had to have a C.P.A. degree if I expected to get anywhere, so I went to night classes at Wayne to qualify for it. Since you explained about the figures, I can see how you knew about the accounting, but until tonight I just never realized that C.P.A.'s and engineers wrote any differently from anybody else. . . .

"Several years ago," he continued, "I invented a formula a bank can use to evaluate the exact profit or loss it makes on a specific account, especially a small one, or one that shows wide fluctuations in balance. Hundreds of banks across the country have adopted it, and as a result I've had lots of invitations to speak at meetings, just as you said. I put some of these speeches and lectures together and made a

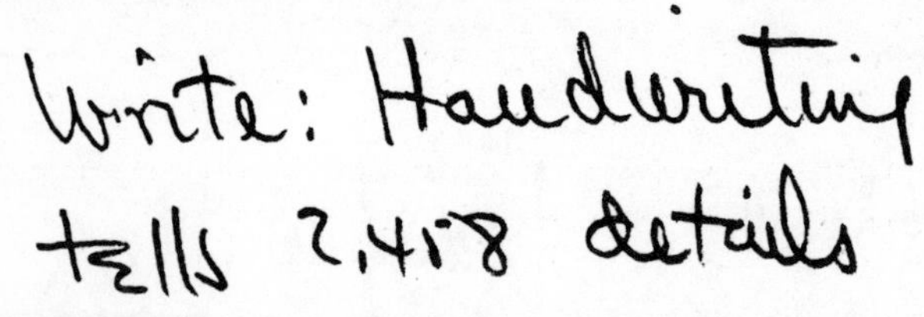

8-21 120° CHOOSY: engineer turned financier, in export-import business; champion swimmer and skater in school, won medals in rifle and skeet; "invents" solutions to financing export-import activities.

couple of textbooks out of them. My own alma mater is now using one of them in its classes. When you said my writing showed I had inventiveness and that I could be successful in research or lecturing or writing books about financial and accounting subjects, I looked all around the room to see if there was anybody here that might have told you who I am—but there isn't."

I assure you this experience is literally true, but if I were a fiction writer I could not have imagined a character who would be a more accurate example of the type of personality and occupation you would expect to find in an intelligent man who wrote with an average slant of 120° CHOOSY.

10) 130° CHOOSY. The same pattern as described above holds true for persons in this category, except that here we are in the area of management rather than finance. Here you are likely to find a management consultant, or a research worker, a lecturer or writer on managerial subjects. This person might be a department head, a professor in a graduate school of business, or one who works out

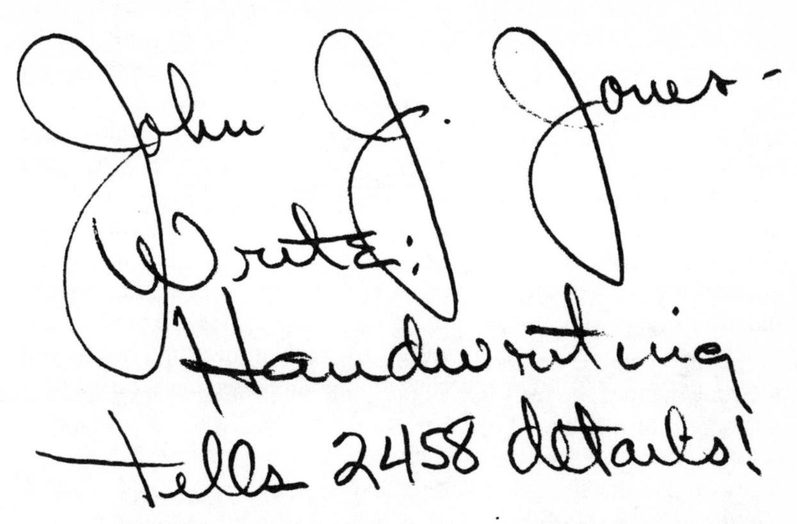

8-22 130° CHOOSY: ex-president of corporation, now partner in management consulting firm; lectures on this at conventions and colleges.

scientific tests to determine whether an individual possesses executive traits. If the script shows a little more energy, creativity, or flair for the dramatic, then this person might do well as the general manager or owner of an advertising and public relations agency or as the stage manager, professional director, or producer of shows, on or off Broadway.

A woman who writes a consistent backhand, especially if its slant is 130° or more, is a natural-born actress, even if she has never set foot on any stage. She will be CHOOSY in many different ways. She is often alone without being at all lonely; in fact, she must have privacy,

8-23 130° CHOOSY: movie director.

a boudoir where she can get away from everybody, even members of her own family whom she loves dearly. She is choosy, selective, particular and finicky about anything *she* considers important: a wedding dress for herself or her daughter, a school for her children, the hat she will wear on Easter, a house to live in and the furnishings for that house, including the husband who will share it with her.

If she has to go to a party for social or business reasons (often it's her husband's business reasons), even if she doesn't like a single soul at the party and is bored with the whole affair, she can appear to be having a good time and can say so convincingly to her hostess. This is the equivalent of the "act" put on by a performer who receives a telegram saying her mother is dying, but who goes out front to play the comedienne; she feels one emotion on the inside but convincingly portrays a quite different one on the outside. Of course, if she cannot do this, she certainly is not an actress.

Again let me warn you that the pressure is very important in making an actual interpretation. A woman who writes this degree of backhand, with a pressure of at least #6 or greater, may actually be an actress or performer of some type, such as a model, dancer, or musician; or she may be a hair stylist, fashion coordinator, dress designer, or interior decorator. If the pressure in the writing is about #3, she may well do any of these things as a hobby, or merely in the privacy of her own home, but she never gets around to doing the tremendous amount of work it takes to make a living out of these activities.

And if her writing pressure is only #1 or less, she is simply a dreamer. She thinks it would be "nice" if she could learn to paint, play a musical instrument, or design and make a dress for herself, but she is so "busy" she never finds time to do any of these things. If circumstances compel her to earn a living, she drifts into the first job available, however unsuitable to her talents, and then finds fault with every single condition of her work; the hours, the boss, the position of her desk, and those catty "other people" whom she must endure for eight long hours every day. A woman in this category is not necessarily lacking in generosity; often she will donate substantial sums to foreign missions or to other causes, but would she personally go out to nurse a sick servant who lived in a cottage on the rear of her land? Never!

In seeming contradiction to this, I have found that many professional nurses and some doctors do write a distinct backhand. My interpretation is that these people have a yen for the spotlight but in

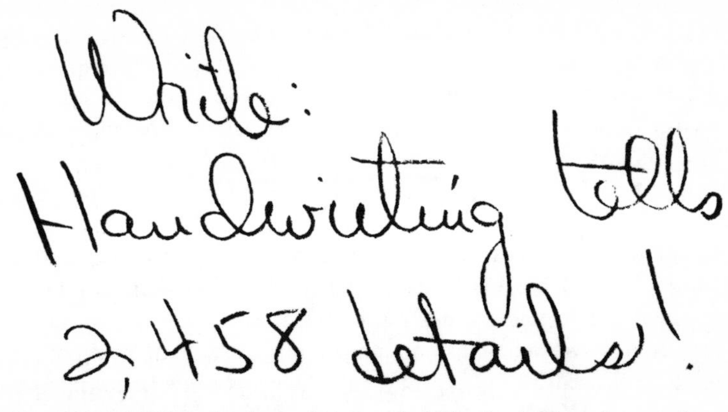

8-24 130° CHOOSY: free-lance designer of children's clothing; she uses her own children as models for ideas.

their opinion they lack the talent required to become a star of stage or screen, so they dramatize their profession by imagining they are another Florence Nightingale, Sister Kenny, or Ben Casey. If they do show a warm, friendly, considerate professional attitude, this is just a deliberate pretense, though it may often be very well done.

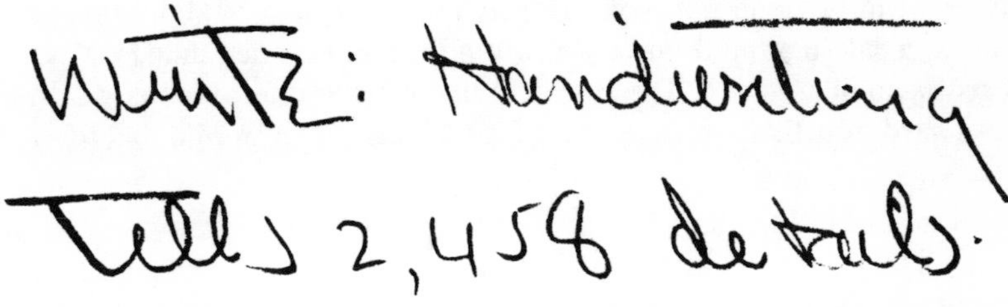

8-25 140° CHOOSY: professional singer turned radio-TV expert for an advertising agency; plays piano (preferably jazz); was "stroke" on champion college crew and expert rifleman medalist in the Army.

11) 140° CHOOSY. Persons whose writing slants average 140° CHOOSY frequently have jobs such as advertising, sales promotion, and publicity directors for big corporations, or they may be executives in areas that range from dressing shop windows to planning exhibits or demonstrations at big conventions. Women who make a business of putting on fashion shows often write with this degree of slant, as does such a person as a former auctioneer who now owns a business that provides auctioneering services in various fields.

In other words, people in this category frequently show executive ability for organizations whose selling is done not face-to-face, but indirectly to audiences or through shows, radio, TV, billboards, display ads, brochures, other mediums of print, and so on. For instance, when one of my clients made a handwriting specimen for me with this 140° CHOOSY slope, it had heavy pressure and showed much creativity, but his long *t*-bars and phonetic spelling indicated that he was ear-minded. Naturally I told him he was well fitted to be an executive in an agency specializing in advertising through the use of sound. He promptly handed me his business card, which showed that he was director of the television and radio division of one of the nation's largest advertising agencies; no jingle, no musical or spoken commercial is released by that agency until he gives it his final approval.

12) 150° CHOOSY. In this class, in general, we find those who tend to deal with things rather than people; in the field of selling, for example, men who compose letters for direct-mail soliciting. Persons who write books, give lectures, teach classes, make phonograph records and tape recordings, or dream up slogans that will help others to sell face-to-face frequently write at this angle.

This gives us one answer to the question so often thrown at instructors who teach salesmanship to trainees in mutual fund, life insurance, or real estate companies' classes: "If you know so well how it ought to be done that you can teach us to do it, why don't you go out as a salesman and make yourself a lot more money than you can earn as an instructor?" The answer is that often it is as psychologically awkward for these men to sell face-to-face as it would be for a

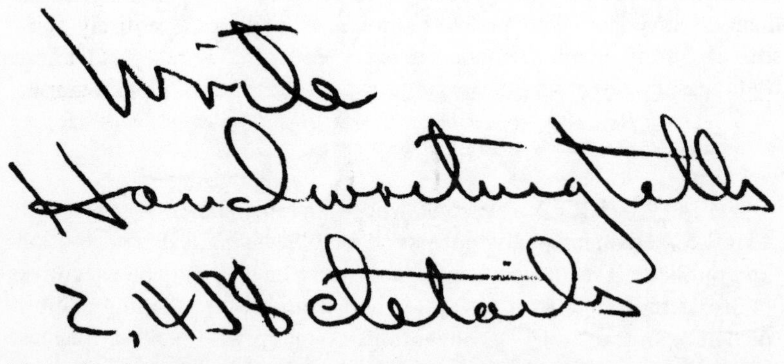

8-26 150° CHOOSY: star salesman turned investment counselor; now partner in brokerage firm specializing in municipal bonds; he does research on their investment quality.

right-hander to start doing with his left hand everything he now does with his right one.

Relatively few men who write a backhand slant of 130°–160° CHOOSY can make a living by face-to-face selling, but those who do are usually extraordinarily good at it. I would not recommend that a man of this type even try such selling unless his pressure is #6 or heavier. Furthermore, this type of person is primarily an actor; he will be successful precisely to the extent that he can learn, by observation or by creative imagination, exactly how a star salesman in his particular line would dress, walk, and talk.

He is most likely to be successful by selling to an audience, like an auctioneer; by demonstrating a machine, like a vacuum cleaner or a typewriter; by working at an exhibit or a display at a big convention; or even by working as a pitchman at Coney Island or Atlantic City. He does not really have to be "sold," himself, on the value of the product he pushes; men who peddle phony mining stocks and other "Blue Sky" items are likely to be of this type. Such a man rarely does well in a field where he must call on the same customers every month or every week, because his great show of solicitude for the buyers' welfare is purely an act, and sooner or later the customers will find out it is only an act.

This type of man is essentially the male counterpart of the famous actress who writes a similar backhand script. After about the fifth curtain call on her opening night she says heartwarmingly: "Thank you so much. You've been a wonderful audience. I love you, I love you, I love you every single one!"

Of course she does not love any one of them at all; she only wants them to love her. The great emotion she displays is entirely self-seeking. If any one in the audience is misled by her words, just let him try to see her in person for ten minutes for an interview, an autograph,

8-27 110°–120° CHOOSY: actress who projects love to audience but is completely self-centered.

a picture, or just to renew a childhood acquaintance; unless he can guarantee in advance enough good publicity to pay her for her time, he will never get within a hundred yards of her.

13) 160° CHOOSY. At this point, and especially when the average slant is somewhat greater than this, you begin to get into the fringe of eccentrics and "odd-balls." If they do show creativity in their scripts, then as artists or writers they frequently tend toward the bizarre. If they have enough intelligence to go with their creativity, they may well be geniuses in some area of their work. To illustrate, let me tell you a true story.

While working in Pittsburgh years ago, I analyzed the writing of each of eight or ten men gathered at one table. Later I learned through one of them, who became a repeat client, that they were all executives of a big coal company and had come down together from a meeting held on one of the upper floors of the hotel. Each one's particular job fitted neatly the precise category of his writing, as described above, so I had no trouble in making accurate analyses.

One of the group was a complete individualist. He showed great drive and creativity, and I estimated his intelligence was well into the

8-28 160° CHOOSY: advertising man who does painting as a hobby.

genius rating, and I told him so. His writing was definitely an action-minded type, with great speed and #8 pressure; all of it leaned distinctly backhand, with an average of about 160° CHOOSY, but with many letters measuring at 170°. I told him: "In business your proper spot is to run an advertising agency or to be advertising and sales promotion manager for a big corporation. But you have a great deal of artistic talent and you should do well in abstract or modernistic painting in oils as a hobby, if not professionally."

A week or so later one of the men at that table came back to see me, this time alone. This is the gist of what he told me then: "Hal, do you remember Larry, the one you said wrote 170° CHOOSY? Well, you didn't make a single mistake about any of us, but you startled me in particular by what you said about him. No one else in the company knows it, but under an entirely different name Larry is one of the greatest modernistic painters in America. Three of his works have been bought by the Museum of Modern Art in New York, and several other big museums have one or more. He gets really fantastic prices for his pictures. He is the advertising manager of our company, just as you said. He hates it every minute but he does a wonderful job of it. I know about all this because Larry is my first cousin; his father is the biggest stockholder in our company, otherwise Larry wouldn't work for us at all. Maybe I'm prejudiced, being a relative, but I think he is truly a genius in both fields, in advertising and in art. He must have been worried when you told him he should be a painter, because he is a fanatic about concealing his interest in art from everybody he knows in the coal business."

Here you can see that the basic principles I am giving you for interpreting handwriting will tell you things about a person that even his best friends do not know. Sometimes the person's subconscious mind will reveal to you in this way things that his conscious mind does not know about himself.

Chapter 9. How Do You Write Your Name?

Men who have achieved any degree of fame as writers or lecturers, or both, frequently write their names in full; that is, all three names are spelled out in the signature; for instance, "Ralph Waldo Emerson" and "Norman Vincent Peale." Years ago I met a man who has since become a personal friend whom I admire a great deal. When he wrote his signature he wrote out three names, "Phillip Roger Morgan" (as I will call him here); but when I asked if he had another form of his name he wrote "P. R. Morgan" very rapidly without ever lifting his pencil. During the analysis I told him that the first signature meant he was probably a writer or lecturer or both and the second signature was that of a business executive, such as a vice-president or a president of a corporation.

Talking with him after the analysis, I learned that both points were precisely accurate: he is the vice-president of a large management consultant association in New York, but he is also a well-known writer and lecturer, a fearless economist who heads his company's research department and produces a variety of learned papers.

Professional men, especially attorneys and physicians, tend to spell out the first name, put an initial for the middle name, and spell out the surname in full. Often this kind of signature is forced upon these men by their profession. In many states a doctor is required to register precisely this form of signature with state authorities and to use exactly the same form on every prescription that he gives. Similarly in some states lawyers are required to use this form of signature on all legal transactions and documents. Such a man then would tend to use this signature on all business letters and on his checking account even though his first name is one his family and friends never use in addressing him personally.

To a somewhat lesser extent other professional men, such as college professors, C.P.A.'s, and engineers use this form of signature. However, if a college professor attains enough stature or fame to become a head of a department, a dean, or a professional lecturer in addition to his teaching position, then he frequently starts writing all three of his names; for example, "Henry Wadsworth Longfellow" and "John Crowe Ransom," both college professors who attained fame as poets.

If, when I ask a client to write his name, he signs such a form as "Bob Smith" or "Jim Jones," it almost always indicates that he is a traveling salesman. In effect, this form of signature represents the attitude of the salesman who told me in answer to my polite "How do you do, Mr. Smith?": "Mr. Smith is my father. Just call me Bob." Such a man wishes to get immediately on a first-name basis with his customers and therefore uses the informal nickname rather than his legal name.

Some people regard a name that is "parted in the middle"—an initial is used, followed by a given name and then the surname—as a sign of a showoff. My experience does not confirm this. Many persons write a signature such as "J. Robert Smith" simply to avoid getting their checks, mail and telephone calls mixed up with those of the other Robert Smiths who live in town. In other cases the man has always been called by his middle name, so naturally this is the one he uses in his signature. Sometimes the middle name is an old family name of considerable distinction; for instance, it is understandable that a man might prefer to sign his name "H. Cabot Lodge" rather than "Henry C. Lodge." This practice is particularly common among the states of the Old South.

I have found that in the United States an unmarried woman will usually give her name as simply "Mary Smith" or perhaps "Mary Jane Smith." After she is married to, for example, a Mr. Jones, she should write her name legally as "Mary S. Jones" and not as "Mary Jane Jones" or "Mary J. Jones," although I have frequently found the latter form in use. In this country it is relatively rare for a woman who has never been married to write her name with a middle initial; if she does so, and if she looks to be beyond the age of twenty-five, I would immediately assume that she was a widow or a divorcée, even if she were not wearing a wedding ring. However, if a woman practices law in the United States under her maiden name, then after she marries it is customary for her to hyphenate her surname with her husband's; for example, "Mary Jane Smith-Jones." If she continues to practice law after she is married, this is almost a business necessity, since otherwise former clients might not be able to locate her.

The simplest form of signature for a businessman, of course, is simply the two initials followed by his surname. By the time he gets high enough in rank to have a title or to be head of a department, he usually must sign so many bulletins, memos, and letters every afternoon, that he cannot take time to spell out even a short name like "Roy" or "John" in addition to his last name. And as he moves up the ladder of success, the number of signatures per day increases until the

9-1

three initials become a monogram and the last name, a series of illegible wiggles, all written without lifting the pen from the paper. Thus, in a big corporation it is almost axiomatic that the higher the position, the less legible the signature. I call this last type—the monogram followed by an often illegible scrawl written without lifting the pen—a "connected" signature, and it almost infallibly indicates that the writer has worked up to be a vice-president, president, general manager, or perhaps the owner of a considerably large business.

For example, Figure 9-1 shows the signatures of four executives, listed in alphabetical order, each the top man in a huge corporation. One company produces records as part of a show-business organization, and its president is himself one of the outstanding musicians of our day. His signature gives evidence of his "musical ear."

The other men are all heads of big hotel chains, but with quite different backgrounds. One started as a garbage boy and worked his way up through the restaurant department; he spent decades studying the food that went into his customers' stomachs. Both these phases of his history show in his signature.

The other two men were at the top of their own companies from the beginning; each bought a single hotel and then another and another, until he became the owner of dozens. One started as a partner in a tiny bank and later bought a "glorified apartment house" at auction just as a speculation in bankruptcy real estate; its prompt financial success led to his buying others on a similar basis. I would classify this man as a financial genius who, almost by accident, got into the field of hotels and subsequently accumulated a fortune. His partnership set up an investment trust that later grew into a seventy-million-dollar mutual fund with a thirty-year growth-plus-profits record that eclipses almost all others. His hobbies include the writing of an astute essay on "Controlling Business Cycles" and the composing of songs with danceable rhythm as smooth as that shown in his signature.

The other of these four men learned salesmanship while he was a child by dealing with the customers in a boardinghouse run by his family. He has always been noted for his skill in operating hotels, which are frequently in buildings owned by other corporations, and he has built a worldwide organization on this basis. While his entire career necessarily involves financial shrewdness, the natural traits shown in his signature are those of a chief executive in a "selling" business; a hotel empire certainly fits this description.

Another form of signature very often written by business executives is one that is underlined once or twice; particularly if one of the names has a *y* or *g* in it and especially if it ends in such a letter, the lower loop of the *y* or *g* will be elongated so as to underline the entire name with one or two strokes. Sometimes an initial such as a *C* or an *L* or the last two strokes of an *r, n,* or *m* will be elongated so as to form one or two lines under all or most of the name. I call all of these forms the "Horatio Alger" or "self-made man" signature; it usually indicates a person who has started at the bottom and worked his way up to a position of considerable importance. Such a signature represents basically the same feeling as that of a politician running for re-election who says, "I take my stand on my record"; in other words, he feels he has already achieved enough that he can be justly proud of his accomplishments.

When there are two lines under the signature, I consider that the longer or larger or heavier one nearly always represents a business or professional achievement, such as becoming president of a chamber of commerce, school board, or luncheon club, or perhaps being a consistent winner of golf tournaments.

In almost all Latin-American countries and in some European countries, such as Spain, almost all business and professional men use a flourish that consists of one or more underlinings of the signature. To this extent the line or lines under the signature have much less significance than they do in the United States, but in these Latin countries merely to be a business executive or a professional man is in itself a much greater achievement among the population as a whole than it is here. It has been my experience that in this country professional men, such as lawyers, doctors, and engineers, very rarely underline their signatures unless they are also business executives; a lawyer who is chief counsellor for a big corporation, for instance, or a physician who has become medical director for a life insurance company is likely to underline his name.

All of the above of course is based on empirical data. What follows now is based on a good deal of common sense and behaviorism psychology, plus observation from years of experience in analyzing signatures. If the entire signature is written in a script noticeably larger or with noticeably greater pressure than the sentence in the writing, or if all the initials in the name are noticeably larger, wider, more flourished, or written with heavier pressure than the capital letters in the rest of the script, I take this to mean precisely the same as a big line under the signature; namely, that the person feels that he has "arrived."

9-2

Here are seven signatures (again, the order is alphabetical) of hotel executives whose occupations vary from resident manager of one hotel to senior vice-president of a whole chain. These men move onward and upward so fast that if I stated the title of each one, the information would be outdated by the time you read this. However, one of them, after working his way up from bellman to vice-president and general manager, has left the hotel business to become an associate in a firm of interior decorators that specializes in schools, hotels, libraries, hospitals, and other institutions. According to his signature, he is that one of the seven on this list best suited for such an organization. (Figure 9-2)

So convinced am I that the oversized signature or oversized initials in the signature are a sign of self-confidence derived from satisfaction with past achievements that if I were sales manager for a large company I would never hire as a salesman a man who did not consistently and habitually write his name or all of his initials, or at least the initial of the name by which he was called, with noticeably greater emphasis in size, width, or pressure than that with which he wrote the capitals in the rest of his letter of application.

If only one of the initials—it is usually the middle one of three—is written noticeably smaller, lighter, or narrower than the others, it almost invariably means that the writer dislikes his middle name for some reason. It might stand for a name like "Aloysius" or "Percival," and his classmates may have ridiculed him about it when he was merely a schoolboy. It might be the name of an uncle or some other relative he learned to dislike as a child and whose name he therefore resents bearing.

If the initial of the surname is emphasized by height or otherwise, as compared with the initials of the given names, this indicates that as a child the writer was overly impressed with the importance of the family ancestry or, more immediately, with the importance of his father or grandfather.

The experience I have had with one particular client illustrates the significance of the size of initials. This man came to see me a dozen times at intervals of a week to seven months, but the script that he wrote that very first time, despite the fact that he had been drinking heavily all day, indicated that he was undoubtedly an architect. Other characteristics of his handwriting indicated an intelligence that was near genius, or better, and tremendous creativity. I told him all this, but added that the relatively small personal initials, compared with the huge initial of his family name, showed that as a child it had been impressed upon him what a great family he was born into or, perhaps what a great man papa or grandpapa was. Even at the age of forty (which I estimated he was from looking at him) he was still doubtful that he was worthy of being a member of such an important group. I told him his drinking was probably an effort to escape from these feelings of unworthiness.

After I had finished my analysis, we chatted for nearly an hour and he told me the following: he had been a brilliant scholar in high school and college and had been top man in his class when he graduated with a degree in architecture. During his two years of study in Paris, he had again been an honor student. He had then joined the architectural firm of which his father was sole owner. He had won several awards in various exhibitions for some of his drawings and designs; but no matter how hard he worked or what he achieved, he was convinced that his father was a greater man than he would ever be, and apparently his mother and other relatives emphasized this opinion. As a result, he had taken to drinking. He was about to lose his job as vice-president in his father's firm because he rarely showed up at the office. His drinking had already wrecked two marriages and was in the process of wrecking the third.

What I said to him was this: "Your father had a twenty-five year headstart on you. You are brilliant, a genius in my opinion, but if we could somehow prove that you are actually 50 percent smarter than your father, you still couldn't possibly compete with him. Your father is certainly a brilliant man, but he will eventually have to retire, and by the time you are as old as he is you will undoubtedly have an even better reputation than he has now—unless you continue to drink yourself to death because you have not been able to accomplish at forty as much as he has, at sixty-five."

Somehow these words got across to him what five years of psychiatric treatment and fifteen years of berating by his wife and family for his drinking had not been able to do. Ten days later he came back to see me, this time with his wife. He made another specimen of his handwriting for me and asked me to tell his wife what I had told him previously. He swore he had not had a drink since our last conversation, and his wife said she thought this was true. At the end of a week in which he had appeared at work regularly in his father's firm, he had called his wife long-distance to persuade her to come back and live with him. I repeated to her the fact that he was badly frustrated because of his inability to compete with his father; I hoped she would remind him of this from time to time and discreetly pass the word along to other members of his family. I also urged him to join Alcoholics Anonymous and I learned later that, although for years he had steadfastly refused, he had done so.

Some five years after our first interview, this man came in to see me, with the same wife, to tell me that on that day, upon his father's retirement and by a unanimous election by the board of directors, he had assumed the presidency of the firm. His wife told me he had won several honors for his designs during the past few years and that he was still "dry" (as the A.A. would put it). She was kind enough to credit my first analysis of his handwriting with having started the entire series of happy events.

Recently, they both came in to see me again, professionally. This time my client wrote a big, illegible, connected signature, but his own initials were noticeably larger than the initials of his surname. His wife told me that his father had died a couple of years after retiring and her husband, being an only child, had inherited the business as a part of the family fortune. But during the time he had been president, the firm had prospered more than it had during any similar period under his father's management. My client's own professional reputation and that of his firm have continued to grow. So this story very definitely has a happy ending.

By a similar application of common sense psychology, a wife who writes her husband's family name, or the initial of it, with considerably greater emphasis than that with which she writes her own initials indicates that she thinks she has married "above her station." Repeated observation of actual cases convinces me that this theory is true. The converse is also true: if a woman writes her husband's surname smaller, or if she writes its initials noticeably smaller than the initials of her own name, she thereby indicates a low opinion of him or his family or both. I have noticed especially that divorcées who have not had their maiden names restored, perhaps because they have children who retain their father's surname, tend to write the ex-husband's family name noticeably smaller, or with less pressure, than their own name. In particular, such women tend to write their former husband's family name with a capital letter for the initial smaller than the initials of their own personal name. All of this, again, subconsciously expresses their low opinion of the man.

Recently I pointed out this fact to a woman client who had been divorced about two years previously, and she flatly denied that it was true. To prove that I was wrong, she pulled out of her handbag a few cancelled checks she had received from the bank that day and several credit cards and driver's licenses that dated back several years. To her own astonishment every signature she had written since she had broken up with her husband, nearly three years previously, showed his family name was relatively small, but every signature written prior to that time showed his family initial slightly larger than her own initials. A week later she came back to tell me that she had been so interested in this discovery that she had gone back to the file of receipts she kept for her income tax records and had looked at cancelled checks written several months or years before she discovered his liaison with another woman.

"I remember the exact date," she said, "because it was on St. Patrick's Day. Being Irish, he had naturally been out celebrating, but he was celebrating with this other woman and not with me. I had never suspected such a thing. When I discovered it the next day, I found that the affair had been going on for several months. So I moved out of the house that very instant and turned the case over to my lawyer. And you know, Hal, the first check I wrote was to pay my lawyer his retainer, and that very check shows the small initial that you pointed out to me."

This woman thought she was praising me for my astuteness, of course, but actually the praise was not due to me personally but simply to the science of graphology. With a little experience you can be just as accurate if you will read and apply the simple common sense principles explained in this book. I mention *experience* because anything new you try to learn—dancing, swimming, ice skating, or riding a bicycle—takes a little practice before you can do it well. Learning to analyze handwriting, however, is much simpler than learning any of these things!

Now let's go back and look at the way you wrote your name according to the instructions in chapter 2. Did you put a period after each of your initials? Did you carefully dot every *i* and cross every *t* in your name? If your signature contains an abbreviation, a *Mrs.,* or a *Jr.,* did you carefully put a period after that abbreviation?

If you did all these things, then you are obviously the type of person who would insist on reading all the fine print in a contract before you would sign it, and you would be just as careful about any other document or action for which you were officially responsible, even if you did not have to sign it. If you were equally careful with the punctuation, *i*-dots and *t*-crosses in the sentences you wrote, then you probably are visual-minded and verge on being a perfectionist. You may even insist on checking and double-checking personally any piece of work that is prepared by someone under your supervision.

If your name shows this meticulous attention to detail but the rest of your writing does not, you probably dislike paper work and should avoid having to prepare such things as inventories, financial statements, expense accounts, or income tax reports. If you do have to prepare such a paper, then you insist that it be very accurately done.

On the other hand, if your signature does not show periods after the initials or other visual details but the sentences that you wrote do show these details, then I would say that you, too, are one who greatly dislikes paper work. Your writing indicates, however, that you have had to do a considerable amount of such work and you have learned to be very accurate in doing it, even though you dislike it. All of this, as you can readily see, is simple common sense applied to the habit formations you show in your handwriting.

Now look again at your signature. If each time you wrote the initial for the name by which you are most frequently called you made it considerably wider, larger, or heavier than the other capitals on the page, including especially the initial of your family name, this indicates that you have acquired considerable self-confidence, although it may have been painfully acquired. The larger and more heavily you write your signature and the more you emphasize your personal name or its initial, as compared with other parts of your signature, the more this indicates you have probably overcome original feelings of inferiority. If, in addition, all of your writing and especially your signature, including particularly your personal name or initial, show a considerable amount of pressure, then this indicates that you have devoted much "power" to accomplishing the achievements in the past which now justify your self-confidence.

In some books on graphology you will find that such large initials in your personal name indicate conceit. If you have absolutely no accomplishment to show as a justification for your large initials, then this might be true.

The difference between conceit and self-confidence is explained by this example: if I told you I could run the mile in four minutes, I would be a conceited braggart; I doubt if I could do it in forty-four minutes. But if a man like Herb Elliott tells you he can run a mile in four minutes, his accomplishments show that he is not conceited, he is merely stating a simple fact. He once held the world's record for the mile and has been clocked officially seventeen times in running it in four minutes or less. He is therefore justified in his self-confidence that he can do a creditable job in running not only the mile, but the half-mile, two-mile, or five-mile course as well.

So I interpret your big initial or initials in the same way as meaning that you have accomplished, in your own particular field, things that were just as difficult for you at the time as running a mile in four minutes or less was for a track man the first time it was ever done. Because you have done these things successfully, you are now justifiably confident that you could do them again, or that you could solve equally difficult problems.

In general your signature represents the image of yourself that you wish the world would accept. Followers of Freud would call it the *persona:* the image you present to the world. The rest of your writing will reveal, to one who has studied this book, what kind of person you really are behind what is perhaps the mask of your signature.

If large or emphatic initials do not indicate conceit, then what does? From my experience, I would say conceit is indicated by personal initials that are overly flourished or obscured almost to the point of illegibility by lines that are not actually needed to form parts of the letters themselves. I would consider this interpretation confirmed if the writing, especially the signature, showed little or no pressure. Such a signature would mean the writer wanted to be considered a "big shot," but simply had not put out enough energy to achieve the results required to justify his good opinion of himself.

But now what about the person who writes an unusually small signature or small initials as compared with the rest of the writing? This indicates that he is a modest and unassuming person who does not try to hog the spotlight. A good friend of mine has such a signature, and his style of handwriting, his high school and college scholarship records, and the I.Q. tests he has taken all justify my calling him a genius. He has what a member of one political party once called "a passion for anonymity" and has never held an elective office, but many people consider him the most astute politician in one of the largest states in the country. Years ago he organized and headed the "brain trust" that pushed his employer—at that time an unknown district attorney—into the governor's chair, kept him there through repeated re-elections, and only by the barest mischance failed to make him President of the United States.

This man is now a partner in a big law firm, serves as chairman of an appointed state commission, but still is the much-respected head of the existing brain trust that has achieved both re-election and national prominence for the present governor of his state and may well succeed in putting that official into the presidency within the coming five or ten years. I consider him a much smarter figure in both state and national politics than is that governor himself, yet he avoids publicity completely and, outside of a few of the inner circle, he is virtually unknown. If you met him or talked with him or looked at his handwriting or signature, as I have done on many occasions, you might well think that he was just a small-town, country lawyer, which indeed he was originally, many years ago. I might add that his writing shows a persistent pressure of #3, whereas the governor mentioned writes with #8 or heavier.

Signing your name is an action that is habitual. The particular form of signature you have selected has become a habit, and writing it is an action that tells much about you.

Now I hope you can understand why, in asking for a specimen of your handwriting or of a client's writing, I always insist on at least one or more signatures in addition to a sentence or two. Your signature may be quite different from the rest of your writing; if you analyze the differences between the two according to the principles of this book, it can reveal to you much that you did not already know about yourself. "Know thyself," said Socrates—and this, according to him, was the beginning of wisdom.

Chapter 10. Sex Symbols In Handwriting

The specimen of writing shown below in Figure 10-1 was done by a nymphomaniac. I have good evidence from two people who ought to know: one of the many men who shared her bed and almost became trapped in it, and a woman roommate (actually a cousin, as I learned later) who shared an apartment with her for more than three years. Perhaps no court of law would consider this admissible evidence, coming from me. But if you ever meet a woman whose writing shows such a long-tailed *y* or *g,* with the varied slants that show confusion, the almost vertical ones that show a really "cold, cold heart," and especially a letter that shows a mental condition, like the *I* (marked with the arrow), then run—don't walk—to the nearest exit and don't come back as long as she is there, or be prepared to take the unhappy consequences.

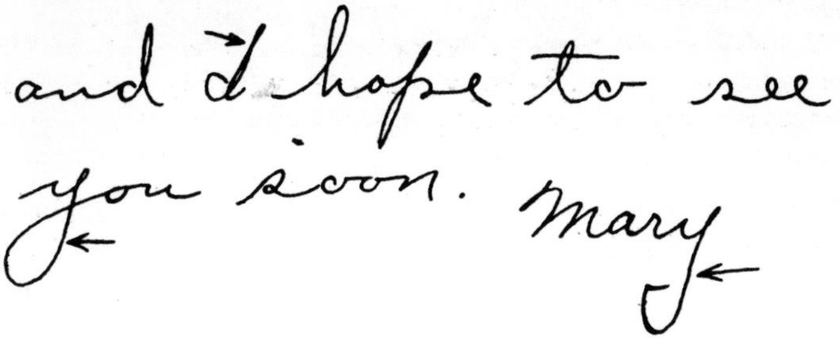

10-1

Since I have mentioned "oversized" tails on a *g* or *y,* perhaps I had better tell you what is normal size. According to the penmanship books, in general, the loops below the line of writing should equal those above it, in such letters as *b, d, f, h, k, l,* and *t.* If you will measure in a straight line from the highest point to the lowest point of all of these letters, in any one specimen of writing, and compare the average of these measurements with the length of the lower-loop letters measured in the same manner, this is your basis for comparison. If the tails of the *y* and *g* average 10 percent or more greater length than the upper letters, I would call them oversized; the more they exceed this percentage, or the more they are emphasized in other ways, such as having inflated loops or noticeably greater pressure, the larger the amount of sex urge this indicates, according to my experience.

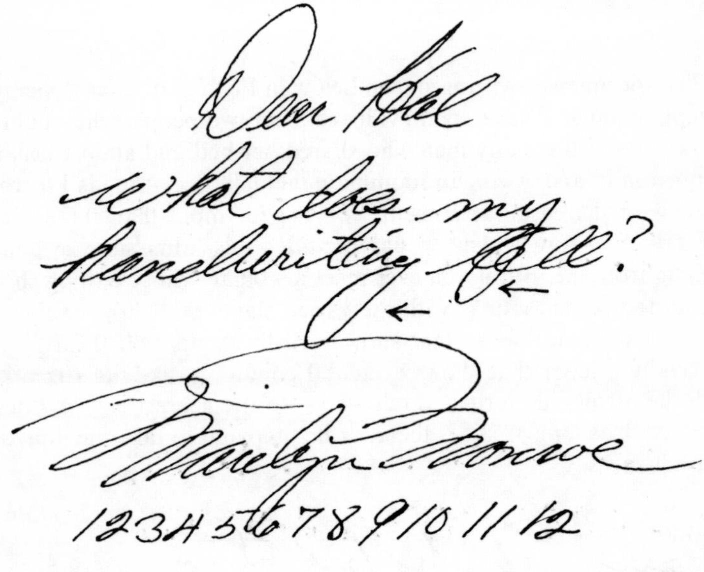

10-2

The writing shown in Figure 10-2 was written by a young woman whose autograph is one of my most valued possessions. It was given to me over a dozen years before her recent tragic death, at a time shortly before the second of her three marriages, when she was soon to become a star so famous as to be proclaimed "America's Sex Goddess." Notice that the *y* has a loop that runs a quarter-inch below the next line of writing, making it by actual measurement (as described above) twice as big as the *l* in *tell;* the *g* in *handwriting* is the same length as the *y* and a similar letter in her name.

As for the slant, my LOVE-ARC measures the *W*, the *a* of *What* and *handwriting*, and the *e* of *does* and *tell* at 155° ARDENT and no letter at less than 140° except the very first one. Do you recall my telling you that persons with writing at such an inclination expressed their emotions toward people and did well in sales work? Do you see, then, how this specimen shows this actress not only felt a powerful sex urge, but was able to express it emotionally as sex appeal and sell that sex appeal in pictures that grossed millions?

10-3

Almost all the specimens I have shown you so far contain only phallic symbols; now I have one for you that contains a huge triangle indicating tremendous interest in the female body. Since the writer is a woman, let me assure you that there is nothing abnormal about this; she was a model for bathing suits who later studied dancing and then singing. Because it was her exceptional beautiful body that gave her a start in show business, it is not surprising that it was as important to her as a Stradivarius is to a concert violinist and that it was so constantly on her mind that a symbol of it shows emphatically in both her signature and her writing.

It is this situation, in my opinion, that causes her subconscious mind to express a very powerful sex urge by an exaggeration of the female rather than the male symbol. Writers who have a sex interest in persons of both genders, or of their own, indicate this in a quite different way, as I will show you later in this chapter.

In telling you previously about Rollo and Julie, I mentioned that Rollo's writing showed frustration, and he confirmed this, explaining that he had not been with his sweetheart for a month because of her trip to Bermuda. There are two other classes of people who would normally suffer sexual frustration that would show in their writing: the religious and the widowed (including the divorced). I have never analyzed the script of a nun, but I have had a dozen or so priests as my clients; on the next few pages I will show you specimens of their writing.

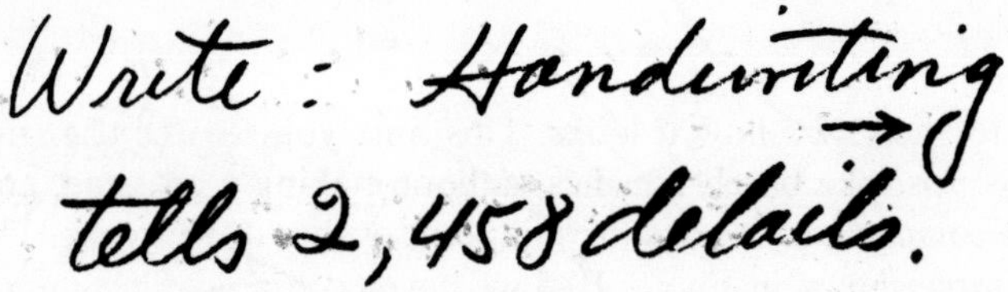

10-4

The script, shown in Figure 10-4, contains a *g* whose length is a trifle greater than the height of the first leg on the *H,* and is therefore 10 percent to 50 percent larger than any other loop letter. Notice that the upstroke on its tail is left unfinished but, had it been completed, the point where it crossed the downstroke would have been about two-thirds of the way up from its bottom. Had this writer made the lines cross in such a location, the relatively long distance that it would occur below the base line of the writing would mean that, to him, it had been "a long time" since he had had sexual satisfaction. The fact that he has left the loop incomplete indicates that he considers his sex life incomplete as, of course, his vocation requires.

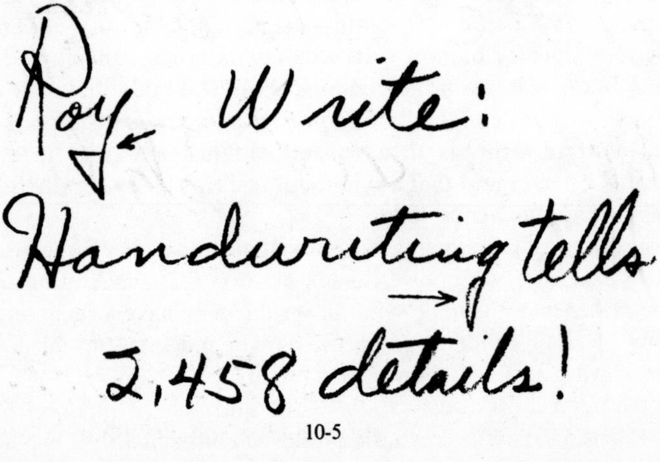

10-5

The script, shown in Figure 10-5, has a *g* just a trifle longer, but the upper-loop letters are taller, too, so the sex drive in this priest seems to be a trifle less powerful. Since the upstroke only touches the downward one, it leaves the loop still unfinished; its closing line lacks a part of the tail projecting beyond where the two strokes meet. The distance from the bottom of the bulb of the *g* to this point of juncture is about one-quarter the distance from the bottom of the loop; again, this indicates that the writer has not had sexual satisfaction for a considerable length of time.

Since this man has a *y* in his name, I have diagrammed the word "Roy" to show you how it looks. This time you see the triangle, but again its upstroke barely touches without making a crossing, and the contact comes barely above the midpoint of that downstroke. Thus in the example shown in Figure 10-5 we have both a phallic symbol and a female one, both showing frustration and "lack of completeness."

The priests whose writing is shown in the above two figures are both husky athletic types of Irish ancestry. When I told the first one that he could be good at putting, he admitted that he was a competent golfer and that putting was the best part of his game (notice the scallops that indicate his coordination). The second priest wrote with such heavy pressure I told him that football and long drives in golf should be among his acomplishments. He said he had won letters in both basketball and football at college and was noted for his ability to "get distance" off the tee.

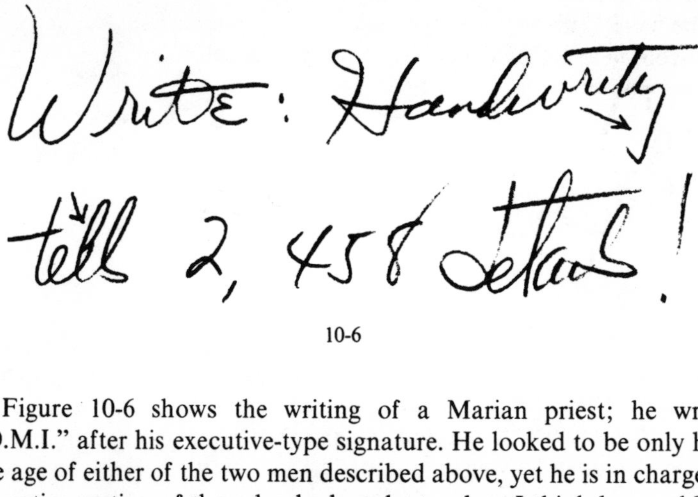

10-6

Figure 10-6 shows the writing of a Marian priest; he wrote "O.M.I." after his executive-type signature. He looked to be only half the age of either of the two men described above, yet he is in charge of an entire section of the school where he teaches. I think he would be called "principal" if it were a public rather than parochial school. His writing has only half as much pressure as that in Figure 10-5 above, and you can see that the *g* has even less relative length and only the beginning of the upstroke. The defect in the *l* of *tells* is not a limp in my opinion, but it indicates haste and absentmindness: he first wrote *teels,* but was too hurried to use the eraser on my pencil, so he just added a loop to make the second *e* into an *l.*

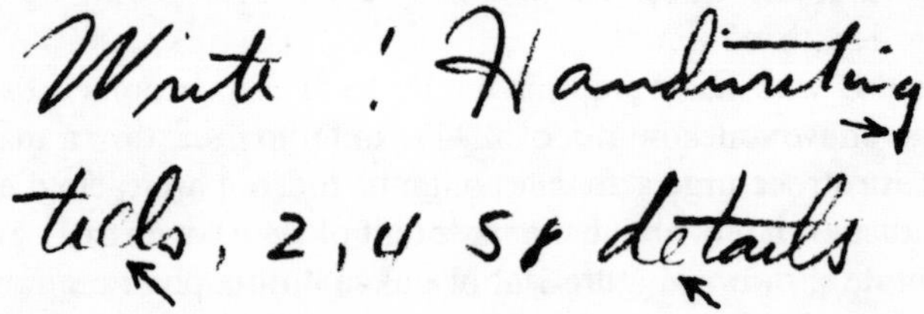

10-7

Figure 10-7 shows the writing of a Benedictine monk who serves as pastor of a church in a small town. He said he had a tendency to be very tense and nervous. Although I did not tell him so, the irregularity of pressure (compare the first with the second *l* in *tells,* and note the pale *e* in *details*) indicates he has some deficiency of energy, so he may have been suffering from low blood pressure or some metabolic trouble. Perhaps for this reason, his libido is not very great, as you can see by the relative shortness of the *g,* which again has only the initial part of the return stroke.

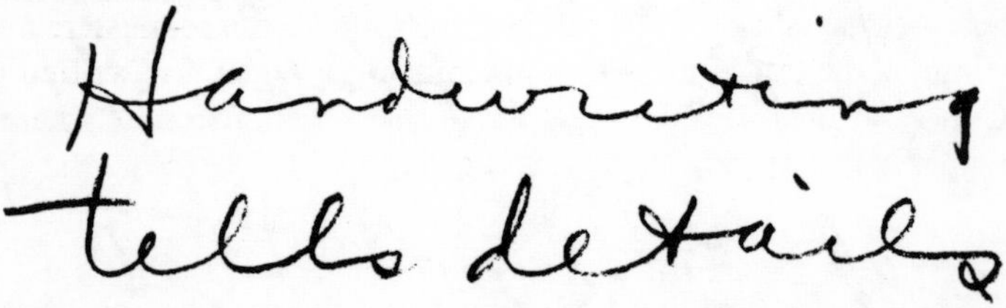

10-8

Finally, here are three secular priests who show very little libido; in each case, the downstroke of the *g* is relatively short, and the upstroke is tiny or, in one script, completely nonexistent. The man who wrote Figure 10-8 writes with #6 pressure, and the stem of his *g* seems even a couple of grades heavier than that. The handwriting shown in Figure 10-9 belongs to a man who was born in Ireland, as his distinct accent

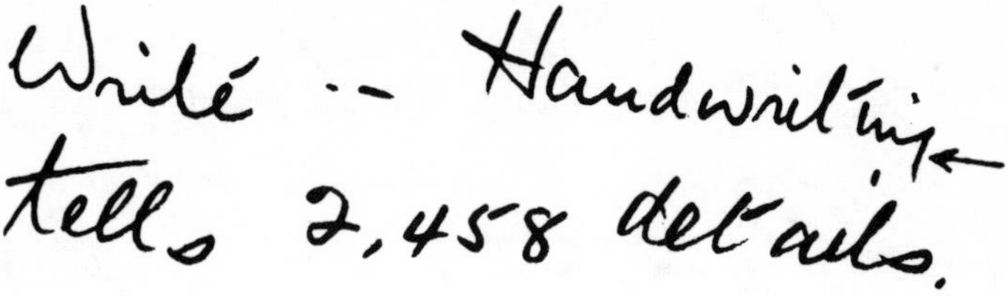

10-9

told me, and who was enroute back there for a vacation when I met him. This priest writes in the manner I would expect from a man who had almost no sex urge at all, although he did not appear old enough to have outgrown it (some men *do* get that old, I have heard!). So girls, if your writing shows a great deal of passion, don't ever marry a man whose writing has a *g* or *y* that looks like this man's. A church can hire an assistant pastor, but in this country a woman is forbidden from hiring an assistant husband to keep her happy in bed.

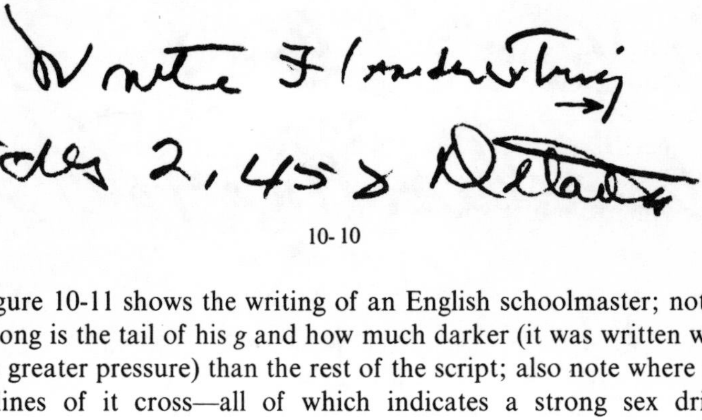

10-10

Figure 10-11 shows the writing of an English schoolmaster; notice how long is the tail of his *g* and how much darker (it was written with much greater pressure) than the rest of the script; also note where the two lines of it cross—all of which indicates a strong sex drive.

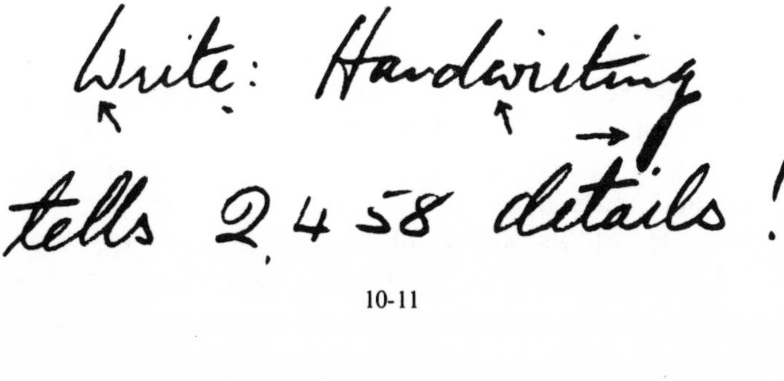

10-11

Handwriting tells 2,458 details!

10-12

A man who is divorced wrote the sample shown in Figure 10-12. The *g* in his script is only a trifle longer than the first *l* of *tells,* but this makes it 50 percent to 100 percent longer than the other tall letters. The *g* is somewhat heavier than the other letters, but notice that the lines cross even below its midpoint. From these observations I would say that this man feels greatly the lack of the sex life his wife should have provided, and he has not yet found a satisfactory substitute.

What does my handwriting tell?

10-13

Another man in exactly the same situation shows his lack by making only two sides of the triangle in his *g* and by omitting the third stroke that would have made it complete (see Figure 10-13). The large, completed loop in the *y* of *my* is somewhat contradictory, however; putting the two together may mean he has found a substitute wife that is halfway satisfactory.

Naturally, passion or frustration will show in the writing of women in a similar manner. Sometimes it appears in the signature, but not in the script. Figure 10-14 shows the writing of a widow who has been married and divorced four times. She owns three ladies' wear stores in one large city, and manages them all herself, although she is nearly sixty-five years old. She didn't tell me she was in a hurry to marry again, but notice the large loops in the two tails of the *y*'s in her name

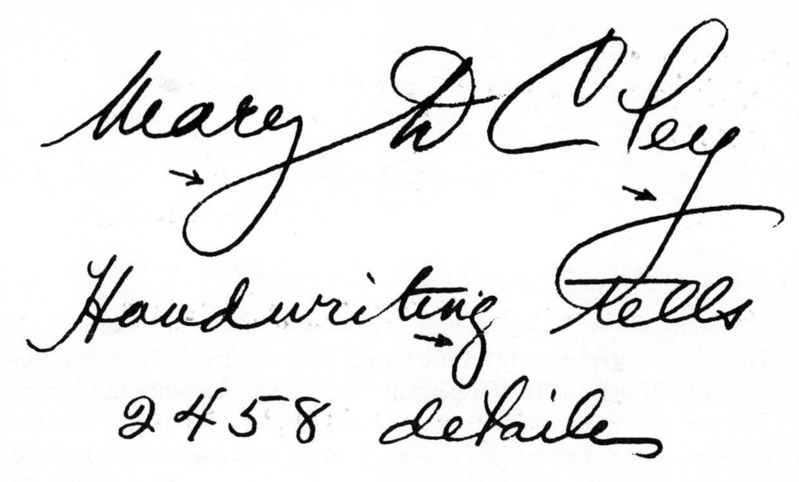

10-14

and the long gap between the crossing and the base line, which indicate quite clearly that she is *"anxious."*

Figure 10-15 shows a sample written by a divorcée in the same situation. As you can see, she is definitely an individualist who craves the spotlight; she does bit-parts on TV and dreams of stardom. But that isn't all she dreams about: look at that exaggerated phallic symbol in the *g*, with the loop crossing just above its midpoint, and notice that she makes another loop between the *l* and *s* of *details.*

Most of the handwriting specimens I have been showing you involve sex symbols in the letter *g* but that is just because the sentence I use for copy has a word that ends with *g*. Other letters, of course, may also carry sex symbols. In Figure 10-15 above there is one

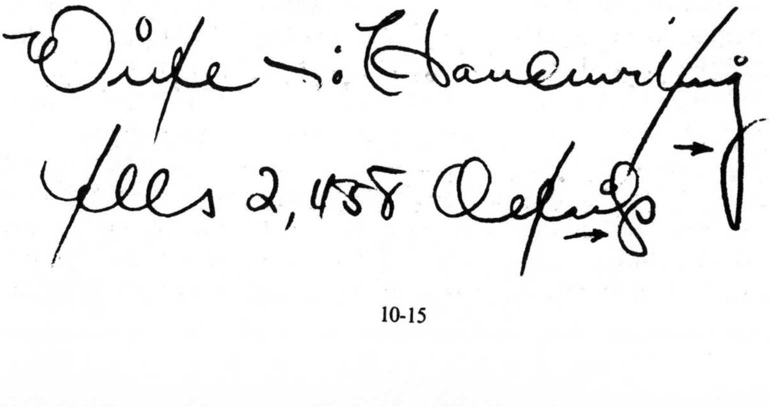

10-15

May
Handwriting tells

10-16

attached to an *l.* You will recall also the *C* and *s* of *Collins,* illustrated in Figure 1-1 of this book. Now look at the *y* in Figure 10-16; it shows a great deal more sexual frustration than does the *g* in the same specimen. This sample was written by a chorus girl who was very attractive and met enough people in her occupation that she could have had her choice of a half-dozen men any night in the week. It is by her own choice that she remains frustrated.

Write: Handwritig
tells 2,458 details!
Amy

10-17

Figure 10-17 shows the writing of a divorcée, a professional dancer who now heads her own dance studio (notice the rhythmic base line). Although she is now middle-aged, she still retains much of her curvacious figure. Since she spends most of every working day in leotards or other costumes that closely outline every inch of her body, her subconscious naturally puts the symbol for it in one of the letters of her own name. The gap between the crossing point and the base line indicates frustration, as you know now. The unusually long terminal stroke underscores her name, indicating her pride in her professional success. The downstroke is just as long as that of the *g* in *writing,* so it is nearly double the length of any other letter. This specimen, thus, shows both phallic and female symbols; I think it is significant, and not accidental, that the female symbol is contained in her own name and the male, outside it.

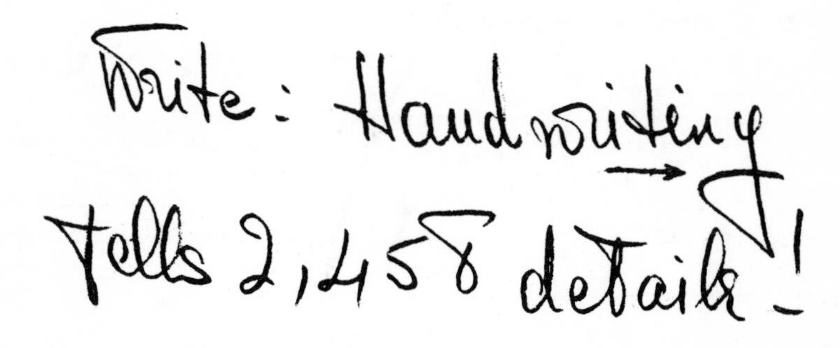

10-18

So far the handwriting I have shown you has all been of Americans; now I will show you the samples of two European women, both of whom are divorced. Since they are foreigners, probably they have never heard of that best seller of a few years back, *How to Live Alone and Like It* (written for single women). They should not buy it in any case because it is obvious they would not—like it, that is. The first of the two women is French and a former model, so naturally the symbol of her frustration is a large triangle placed well down on the stem of the *g*.

The second woman is a Hungarian actress. Her specimen is notable because it contains a *q* (in *queen*) with a downstroke so long it drops below the next base line. I would certainly call this a phallic symbol, as are the *y* in *country* and *nobody* and the *g* in *big*.

Sometimes a widow's writing will show that subconsciously she misses her sex life, but because she is not very passionate she is not too much concerned with its absence. Such a woman is not likely to remarry. Figure 10-20 contains a script that I think is subject to exactly this interpretation: the *y* in the name and the *g* in the sentence are no longer than the other letters, and thus do not indicate more than average interest in sex. The smallness of the triangle in these

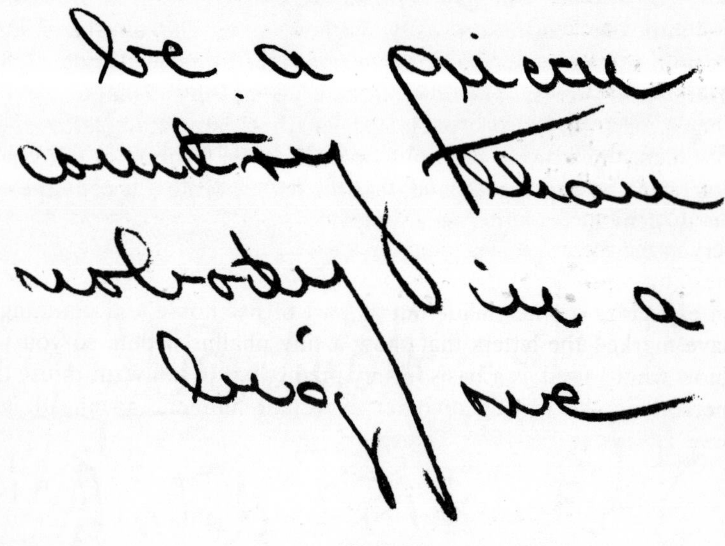

10-19

same letters indicates a lack of interest in the body itself. The incompleteness of sexual relationship is shown by this woman's failure to complete her *g* and by the low crossing point of her *y*.

Phallic symbols, interestingly, are not always an indication of sex urge. One of my colleagues, a very competent graphologist, told me that by means of phallic symbols he can determine from the writing of a pregnant woman, after the fourth month, whether the child she is

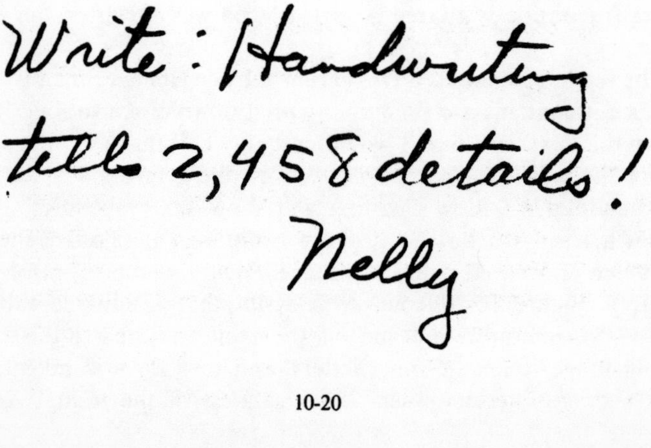

Write: Handwriting
tells 2,458 details!
Nelly

10-20

carrying is male. He says that the mother's subconscious mind is aware of the child's sex and, if it is a boy, will indicate this fact by putting miniature symbols within an *a* or an *o* or similar letters, symbols which do not occur in her normal writing or if the child is female. The theory is interesting. If it is true, then by hypnosis or "truth serum" such a woman could state her child's sex accurately four or five months before birth, since these methods also give access to information contained in the subconscious. Actually I have not had very much success in applying this idea to handwriting, but it did help me win a small bet. Figure 10-21 contains writing from a week's menu an expectant mother made out as part of her household planning. I have marked the letters that show a tiny phallus within, so you will know what I used as a basis for my prediction. If you want to use this method on the writing of other expectant mothers, go ahead: you have at least a fifty-fifty chance of being correct!

10-21

There is little danger of your confusing these tiny phallic symbols with those relating to the libido if you keep in mind that symbols relating to the sex urge are much larger and, as I have shown you, in a different location in the writing. Occasionally, as you have seen, the form of the symbol indicates frustration or resignation. But if priests and persons who have been widowed or divorced show in their writing an absence of sex, there is another group of persons who might be expected to show an excess of it: prostitutes.

On the contrary, all clients I have analyzed who were in this class (so far as I knew), showed the same frustration as widows and divorcées. I take this to mean that the mere physical act of sex, no matter how often repeated, is not sufficient to provide satisfaction; there must be an emotional involvement also.

10-22

Figure 10-22 shows the writing of a woman reputed to be a prostitute. You can see the frustration in the *g;* although it is just a trifle longer than the *t* in the same word, I would say it shows no exaggerated interest in sex. The circular dots on the *i* and the rhythm in the rest of the writing indicate she once had ambitions to be a dancer. When I told her this, she said it was true.

Figure 10-23 contains the writing of a call girl who does show, by the enormous loop on the *g* and by the phallic symbols in the *j* and *y* of her name that she is oversexed, but badly frustrated despite her profession. Officially she worked as a "hostess" in a dance hall in the same block as the hotel where I was lecturing, but she came in so often for dinner with men whom I knew through analyzing their handwriting that I have no doubts as to her real occupation.

The gigantic triangle in *happy* in Figure 10-24, and the phallic symbols in the first *p,* the *g,* and the *Y,* indicate that this particular writer is extremely oversexed; in fact, he is completely bisexual. The script also shows individuality, some "new ideas," and the backhand slant often characteristic of those with an artistic flair. The long *t*-bars and the phonetic errors in the last two words (spelled exactly as in the original) prove him to be ear-minded. As I later found out, this man makes a living creating embroidery designs; he has them put on nylon fabrics in the Philippines and then made up into blouses and negligees and undergarments, which he also designs, and he sells the finished products wholesale in New York City. He has never had a music lesson, according to his wife, but plays the piano beautifully, by ear, reproducing instantly any song he hears on radio or television.

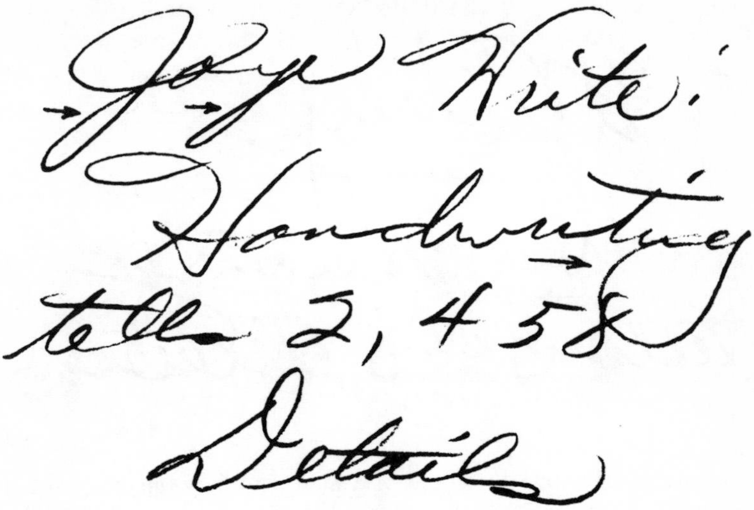

10-23

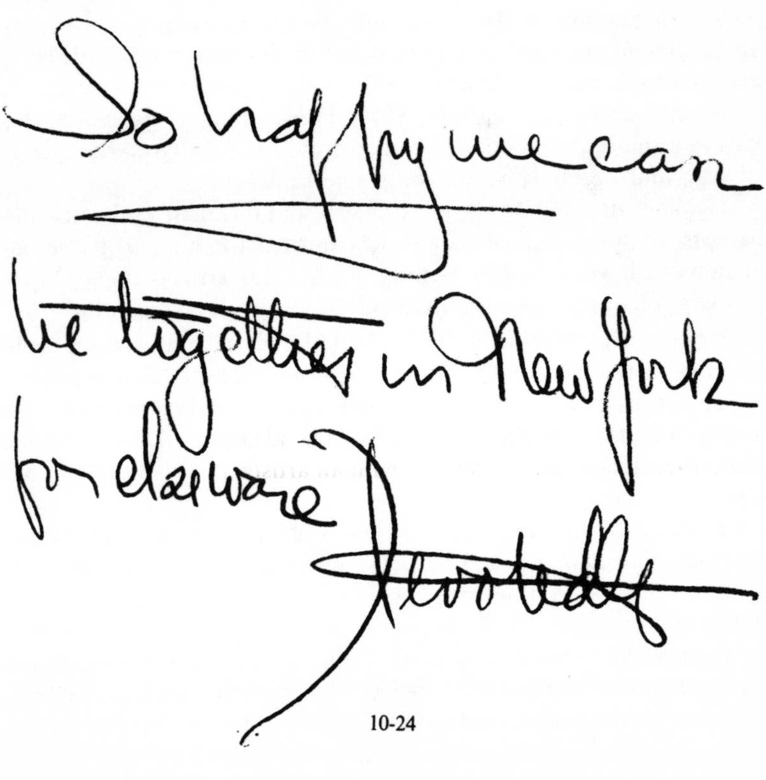

10-24

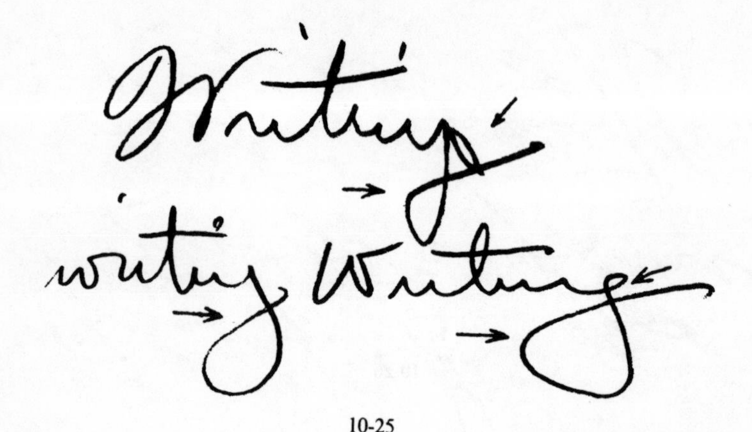

10-25

Figure 10-25 shows the script of a man who may once have been bisexual, but for years he seems to have confined his activities only to his own kind. He himself told me that he once broke off his engagement to a beautiful girlfriend, in order to spend twenty years sharing an apartment with an even more beautiful (to him) boyfriend. He is astonishingly creative. I have read a whole book of his plays in manuscript form, all amazingly good, in my opinion. He can write a play in a single afternoon, faster than I could make a typewritten copy of one, and he rarely revises even one sentence.

The "normal" tail on the *g* may mean that this man's subconscious accepts homosexuality as completely normal for him. In numerous examples I have seen of his writing, I find the oversized loops you see in the *g*, of which there are three on the page, all of them illustrated here. The only oddity I can find in any of them is that the bulb of the *g* in two instances is on the right of the downstroke instead of the left, and that one has no bulb at all. I believe that this indicates haste, but I cannot say for sure; the abnormality at this point in this letter might perhaps correlate with what we consider the abnormality of his sex life.

Next I will show you three specimens in which the loop of the *g* or the *y* does contain unusual shapes, indicating sexual perversion. The writers of these samples are known to be homosexuals (male, not lesbian).

Figure 10-26 shows the writing of a man who recently retired from his position as the art director for a big studio in Hollywood, a position he had held for many years. Observe that the lower loops are

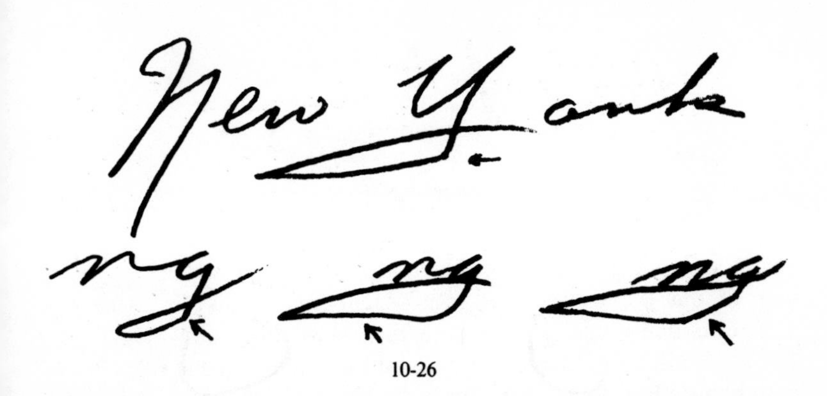

10-26

all exaggerated in size, that one may contain a triangle resting on a side instead of a point, and that all contain a limp (see arrow). In three cases this defect is an angle or point, and in the fourth it is a counter-clock curve, where a clockwise one would be normal. I questioned this man about a possible pain or injury in his right knee or ankle, but he could not remember having had such a thing at any time. The huge phallic symbol in the *Y* indicates he is very much oversexed. The one triangle portrays an interest in the female body, but as far as I knew the only such interest he ever had was in the costuming of the many actresses under his supervision. Perhaps I am stretching a point to get a triangle out of the second of these lower loops; it is quite possible that all four are male rather than female signs.

10-27

The specimen shown in Figure 10-27 is that of a fifty-year-old bachelor who is a famous designer of women's clothing. He too has an interest in the female body, but an interest so slight that he expresses it with an infinitesimal triangle at the bottom of the *g* that is double the length of any other letter he writes. To avoid your having to use a magnifying glass on it, as I did, I have somewhat exaggerated the figure just below the midpoint of the downstroke. I asked this man, too, about an injury in his right knee or calf, but he could not recall

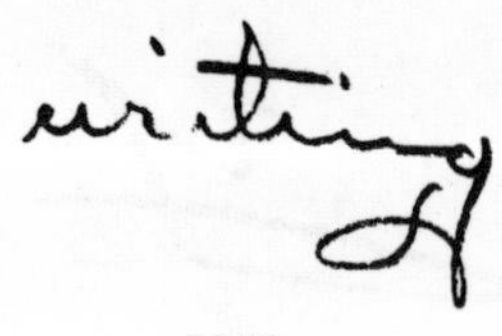

10-28

any. I am forced to conclude, therefore, that the peculiarities in the loop of this *g* correlate with some peculiarity in his sexual desires.

The unique *g* which appears in the handwriting shown in Figure 10-28, is something I have never seen except in this one man's writing, and he used it four times on a single page. It was made by a twenty-four-old TV actor who has sold some manuscripts to his superiors in that field, so I cannot rule out the possibility that this could be considered an "invention" of a new letter-form indicating creativity. If it occurred anywhere except in the tail of a *g* or *y,* or if I did not know this man has a widespread reputation as a homosexual that he does nothing to disprove, I might accept this uniqueness as indicating inventiveness. Under the circumstances, however, I think it is positively an indication of sexual activity that his subconscious mind considers abnormal.

10-29

Figure 10-29 consists of two words from a letter written by a man who is a sadist, unable to enjoy any sexual satisfaction unless he produces noticeable pain for his female partner. What relationship this mental quirk may have to a *g* with a stiff, heavy-pressured downstroke so short that the entire letter could pass for an *a,* I have no idea, but there it is, just as you see it. You will notice, however, that the actual letter *a* in this specimen looks quite different from the *g;* you would never confuse the two in this man's writing.

Perhaps the above examples may inspire some psychiatrist to collaborate by collecting for me sample scripts from his patients, together with a reasonable amount of data about each case. With one or two hundred such specimens, I think it probable we could find correlations accurate enough to be used in making a preliminary diagnosis from the handwriting of a new patient. Thus the doctor would have advance information as to whether masochism, sadism, fetichism, or other abnormalities, perhaps latent, might be uncovered by skillful questioning. I see no reason why phallic or other symbols that occur in handwriting should be considered any less "scientific" than those same symbols that occur in dreams; it is the subconscious mind of the writer or dreamer that puts these signals on display in both instances.

In fact, every illustration in this book pays tribute to the subconscious mind, which is a sort of "third force" in every living person—the conscious mind (which is what you really mean when you say "I" or "me") and the superconscious (which may be a synonym for the religious term "soul") being the other two, of course. It is the subconscious that controls all habits, including the habitual action of writing. You have seen, by samples of actual handwriting, how this habit formation causes a man to write an *H,* a *t,* a 4, or an 8 just the way he learned it in school in a distant country and a different language, sometimes as long as four or five decades before. You have seen how the subconscious puts into writing "limps" that show an illness or defect in a person, of which the writer's conscious mind is totally unaware.

In closing, let me repeat the basic tenet upon which the analysis of handwriting is based:

Whatever characteristics a person shows in one type of action that is habitual, he tends to show these same traits in all other types of habitual action.

Handwriting is an action that is habitual.

Index

Hyphenated numbers refer to illustrations; thus: 1-4 means Chap. 1, illustration # 4.